Ark Signs

That Teach a Flood of Answers

First printing: August 2017
Third printing: February 2018

Master Books®, P.O. Box 726,
Green Forest, AR 72638

Master Books® is a division of the
New Leaf Publishing Group, Inc.

ISBN: 978-1-68344-068-0
ISBN: 978-1-61458-614-2 (digital)

Library of Congress Number: 2017911156

Cover by Diana Bogardus

Scripture referenced in this book is based on the New King James Version, New International Version, English Standard Version, New American Standard Bible, and the New English Translation.

Please consider requesting that a copy of this volume be purchased by your local library system.

Printed in China

Please visit our website for other great titles:
www.masterbooks.com

For information regarding author interviews,
please contact the publicity department at
(870) 438-5288

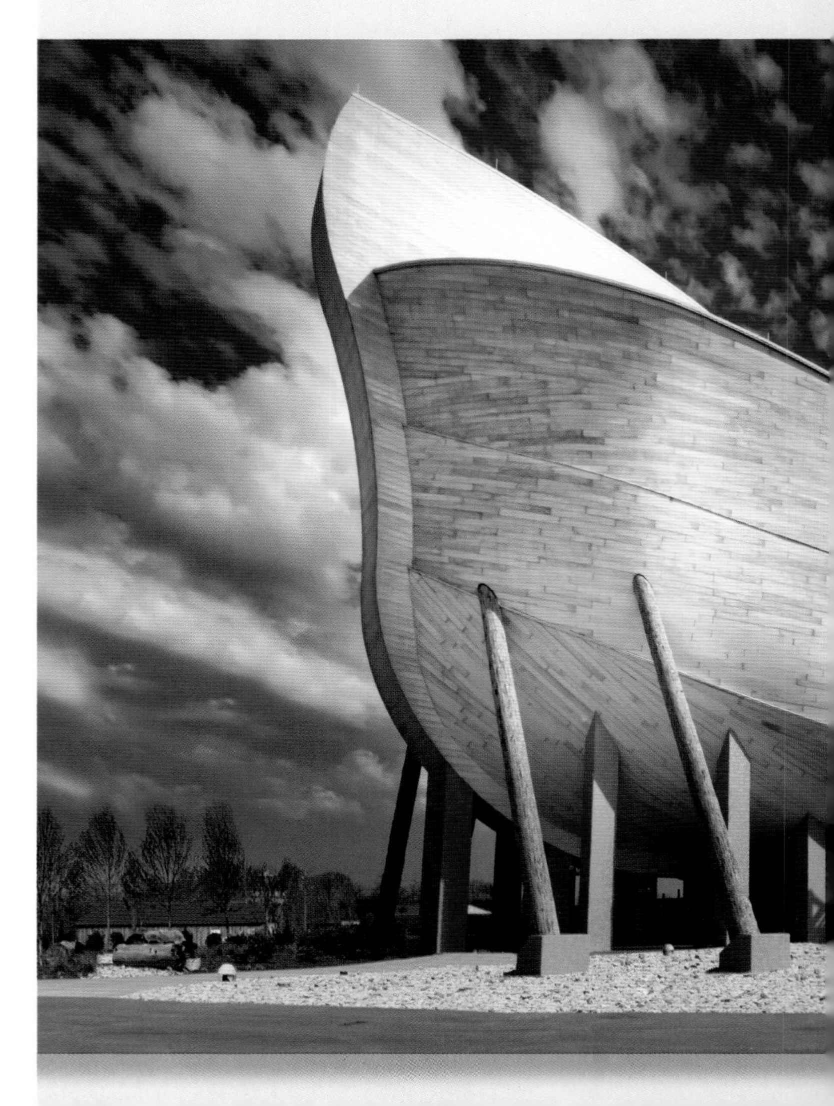

Introduction

The Ark Encounter is a one-of-a-kind attraction featuring dozens of world-class exhibits within its spacious interior. Themed exhibits allow visitors to experience what life may have been like on the Ark. Packed with beautiful artwork, lifelike sculptures, stunning dioramas, and edifying videos, the teaching exhibits in the Ark effectively communicate biblical topics related to Noah, the Ark, the Flood, and most importantly, the gospel message of Jesus Christ.

As content manager for the attraction, I know that each exhibit brought its share of challenges. My assistant, Mike Belknap, and I had the responsibility of writing the text for all of the signage, but each and every display involved many other skilled individuals. We frequently consulted experts in relevant disciplines as we sought to explain a wide variety of complex topics in an easy-to-understand manner. For example, our team often met with Dr. Andrew Snelling (PhD, geology) as we worked on the Ice Age and Flood Geology exhibits, and we checked with specialists in biology and genetics while working on the animal exhibits. All content was thoroughly reviewed by experts before being handed over to our talented graphic designers who transformed our words into attractive signs.

Working behind the scenes with the Ark Encounter's design team was an honor. To have witnessed each of the extraordinary exhibits develop from the initial brainstorming sessions into the finished product enjoyed by thousands of visitors every day at the Ark has been one of the most unique experiences of my life.

Knowing that lives have already been changed for eternity as they have come face-to-face with the gospel message at the Ark Encounter makes all the challenges and long hours we faced well worth it. My prayer is that many more people will come to believe in the Lord Jesus Christ through the teaching at the Ark Encounter and products like this book.

Since we could not fit every Ark sign into a book this size, we selected the primary teaching exhibits for inclusion in this work.

Sincerely,
Tim Chaffey,
Content Manager, Attractions Division of Answers in Genesis

THE STAHLECKERIID KIND

Status: presumed extinct
Adult lengths: 9.8–13 ft (3–4 m)

REPRESENTATIVE SHOWN: *PLACERIAS*

- Better resembling something from science fiction than any animal today, stahleckeriids were a kind of non-mammalian synapsid—being more similar to mammals than modern reptiles.
- Like other stahleckeriids, *Placerias* (depicted here), boasted tusk-like features that were actually facial flanges rather than teeth or true horns.
- The largest known stahleckeriids weighed up to 2.2 tons (2000 kg) when fully grown.

THE CYNOGNATHID KIND

Status: presumed extinct
Adult length: up to 4.8 ft (1.5 m)

REPRESENTATIVE SHOWN: *CYNOGNATHUS*

- Cynognathids and similar groups are considered to be non-mammalian synapsids because they were more like mammals than lizards or crocodiles.
- Cynognathids had opossum-like bodies and may have even sported whiskers.
- The family is named after its only known member, *Cynognathus*, meaning "dog jaw."

THE HYENA KIND

Status: three living genera
Adult lengths: 1.8–5.6 ft (55 cm–1.7 m)

REPRESENTATIVE SHOWN: *ICTITHERIUM*

- Originally classified as dogs, hyenas form a kind of their own.
- The largest known member, *Pachycrocuta*, stood 3.3 feet (1 m) high at the shoulder.
- Wild populations today are only found in Africa and western Asia, but fossil remains have been found in places like England, Java, and Mexico.

CANIDS
THE DOG KIND

The figure in this display case is modeled after the extinct canid, *Hesperocyon*. Over 160 fossil specimens of *Hesperocyon* have been collected from Eocene and Oligocene rock layers of Canada and the United States.

Modern wolves, jackals, foxes, and other dogs belong to the family Canidae. Since the members of this family can interbreed they are considered to be of the same created kind. This means that all post-Flood canids descended from the members of this kind Noah brought with him on the Ark.

Canines are the only living canids, but historically there were at least two other major groups: the hesperocyonines and borophagines—the latter of which were the "bone-crushing" dogs of North America.

THE ALLIGATOR KIND

Status: four living genera
Adult lengths: 3.3–39 ft (1–12 m)

REPRESENTATIVE SHOWN: *CAIMAN*

- Alligatorids buried in the same rock layers as dinosaurs were often smaller than most modern representatives.
- Giant fossil caimans recovered from Miocene rock layers of South America, *Purussaurus* and *Mourasuchus*, achieved a maximum estimated length of 39 feet (12 m).
- Crocodilians—alligators, crocodiles, diplocynodonts, gharials, planocraniids, and pristicampsids—may form one created kind, but Ark Encounter researchers separated them to avoid underestimating the number of Ark animals.

THE THYLACOSMILID KIND

Status: presumed extinct
Adult lengths: 2.6–6 ft (80 cm–1.8 m)

REPRESENTATIVE SHOWN: *THYLACOSMILUS*

- Resembling saber-toothed cats, the South American thylacosmilids are instead classified as metatherians—a group that includes marsupials.
- *Thylacosmilus* reached the size of a jaguar, though the other members of the kind were smaller.
- It is believed that female thylacosmilids carried their young in a rear-facing pouch.

THE SIMOSUCHUS KIND

Status: presumed extinct
Adult lengths: 2.5 ft (75 cm)

REPRESENTATIVE SHOWN: *SIMOSUCHUS*

- These crocodile-like reptiles likely used their leaf-shaped buckteeth to munch on plants.
- *Simosuchus* means "pug-nosed crocodile" and refers to the flattened faces characteristic of this genus.
- Some researchers believe that they were fossorial—that is, they burrowed.

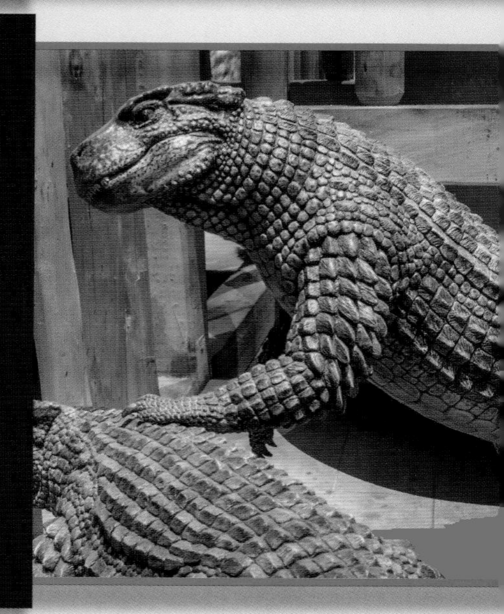

FELIDS
THE CAT KIND

The figure in this display case is modeled after the extinct felid, *Proailurus*. Fossil specimens of *Proailurus* have been collected from Oligocene and Miocene rock layers of Germany, Mongolia, and Spain.

Modern lions, tigers, bobcats, and other cats belong to the family Felidae. Since the members of this family can interbreed they are considered to be of the same created kind. This means that all post-Flood felids descended from the members of this kind Noah brought with him on the Ark.

Living felids are represented by felines and pantherines, but historically there were at least two other major groups: the proailurines and machairodontines—the latter of which were the saber-toothed cats.

THE MACRAUCHENIID KIND

Status: presumed extinct
Adult lengths: 6–9.8 ft (1.8–3 m)

REPRESENTATIVE SHOWN: *THEOSODON*

- The South American macraucheniids are the only known kind featuring both a long neck and facial trunk.
- Like other macraucheniids, our Ark representatives, modeled after *Theosodon*, bore three toes on each foot.
- Macraucheniids had a size range similar to camelids, but are thought to have gone extinct during the Ice Age.

THE SILESAUR KIND

Status: presumed extinct
Adult lengths: 2.3–9.8 ft (70 cm–3 m)

REPRESENTATIVE SHOWN: *SILESAURUS*

- Silesaurs were not true dinosaurs but were a part of a group that included them—Dinosauriformes.
- They were facultative bipeds, meaning they could move on two legs if necessary.
- The largest known member of this kind, *Asilisaurus*, grew up to 3 feet (90 cm) high at the hips.

THE ENTELODONT KIND

Status: presumed extinct
Adult lengths: 4–10 ft (1.2–3 m)

REPRESENTATIVE SHOWN: *ARCHAEOTHERIUM*

- Once considered pig relatives, entelodonts were a unique kind known only from fossils found in pre-Ice Age rock layers.
- Nicknamed "terminator pigs," entelodonts ranged from two to over six feet high.
- Certain entelodonts apparently hoarded their prey in meat caches.

ARCHAEOPTERYGIDS
THE ARCHAEOPTERYX KIND

The figure in this display case is modeled after the archaeopterygid, *Archaeopteryx*. Fossils of *Archaeopteryx* have been collected from Jurassic rock layers of Germany.

Long branded a poster child of evolution, ***Archaeopteryx*** poses no difficulty for biblical creationists. Even many evolutionary scientists now reject the idea that ***Archaeopteryx*** was a direct ancestor of modern birds—a fact that often remains unrecognized on a popular level. There is a deep lack of consensus among evolutionists regarding the origin of modern birds.

New fossil specimens, as well as the way in which some researchers now define birds as avian dinosaurs, have sparked disagreements on how to classify ***Archaeopteryx***. Regardless of how people classify ***Archaeopteryx***, only animals within a created kind are related; and kinds never change into other kinds. ***Archaeopteryx*** was neither a "missing link" nor a hodgepodge of different animal traits. Rather, this creature was a complete, fully functioning, and fascinating bird.

THE CATTLE KIND

Status: nine living genera
Adult lengths: 2.6–15.7 ft (80 cm–4.8 m)

REPRESENTATIVE SHOWN: *MIOTRAGOCERUS*

- Bovine are a very diverse group of animals that include buffalo, bison, and certain antelopes.
- When we see the word *cattle*, we often envision modern domesticated members of the genus *Bos*—cows and bulls—but when extinct forms are factored in, this kind is accurately described as "antelope-like."
- The gigantic Ice Age species, *Bison latifrons*, is the largest recorded representative of this kind, surpassing 2.2 tons (2000 kg) in weight and reaching a shoulder height of 8.2 feet (2.5 m).

THE STEGOSAUR KIND

Status: presumed extinct
Adult lengths: 13–30 ft (4–9 m)

REPRESENTATIVE SHOWN: *HESPEROSAURUS*

- Fossil remains have revealed that stegosaur plates were covered in keratin, the same material as hair and fingernails.
- Plate shapes may have been different between males and females, something called a sexually dimorphic trait.
- Stegosaur spikes, or the "thagomizer," were probably used defensively, as indicated by injuries found on an allosaur tail bone.

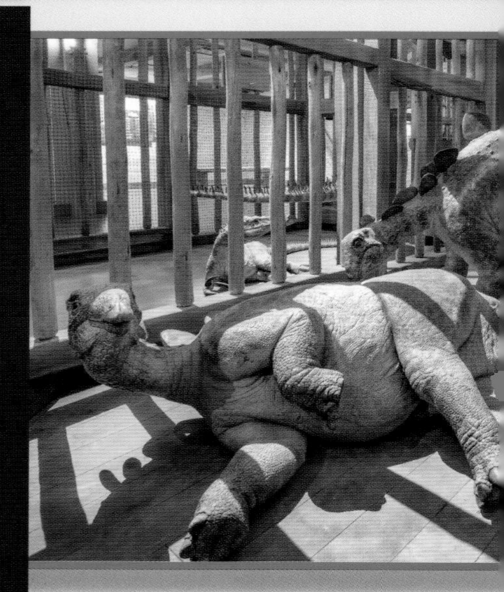

THE PACHYCEPHALOSAUR KIND

Status: presumed extinct
Adult lengths: 4.5–15 ft (1.4–4.6 m)

REPRESENTATIVE SHOWN: *PACHYCEPHALOSAURUS*

- Recognized as the classic "head-butting dinosaurs," pachycephalosaurs weren't born with domed caps.
- Originally considered a unique species, it now seems that *Dracorex hogwartsia* was just a juvenile *Pachycephalosaurus*.
- Broad tail bases likely accommodated a hindgut, while the remainder of their tails were flattened side-to-side and stiffened internally by tendons.

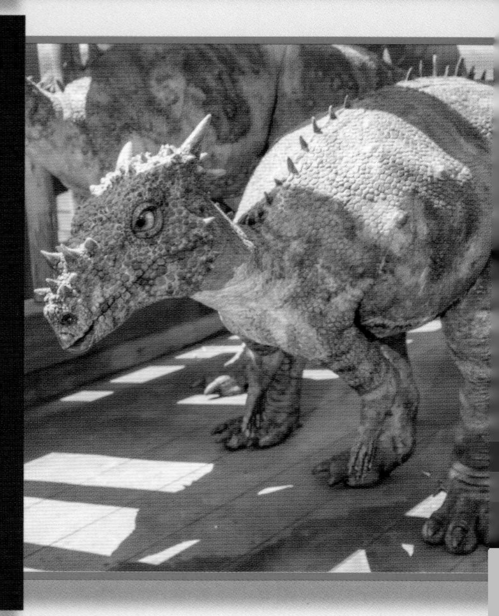

PONGIDS
THE GREAT APE KIND

The figure in this display case is modeled after the extinct pongid, *Pierolapithecus*. Fossils of *Pierolapithecus* have been collected from Miocene rock layers of Spain.

Pierolapithecus is popularly considered the ancestor or near-ancestor of modern apes and humans. But the Bible teaches that the first man, Adam, was formed of the ground and made a living being when God breathed into his nostrils. Furthermore, the Bible teaches that Adam's sin in the Garden of Eden first introduced human and animal death. This means that death—and by necessity, evolution—could not have taken place prior to Adam's sin. Apes and humans are therefore different created kinds.

Some will point to "ape-men" as proof of our non-human ancestry. The problem with this claim is that all of these supposed "missing links" are best identified in one of the following ways: fully humans, fully non-humans, or frauds. Once trumpeted as proof of human evolution, Piltdown Man and Nebraska Man, for example, are now identified as a deliberate fraud and a fossilized pig tooth, respectively. *Australopithecus afarensis* of "Lucy" fame was a chimpanzee-like, tree-dwelling ape, while Neanderthals were the fully human descendants of Noah. So rather than challenging the Bible's claims, these fossil finds are consistent with the scriptural record.

THE SPINOSAUR KIND

Status: presumed extinct
Adult lengths: 25–50 ft (7.6–15.2 m)

REPRESENTATIVE SHOWN: *BARYONYX*

- Spinosaurs were a group of large predatory dinosaurs known for their crocodile-like heads, huge hooked claws, and sailbacks.
- The group is named after its largest member, *Spinosaurus*, who may have spent much of its time in the water.
- At least one representative, *Baryonyx* (depicted here), did not sport a sail.

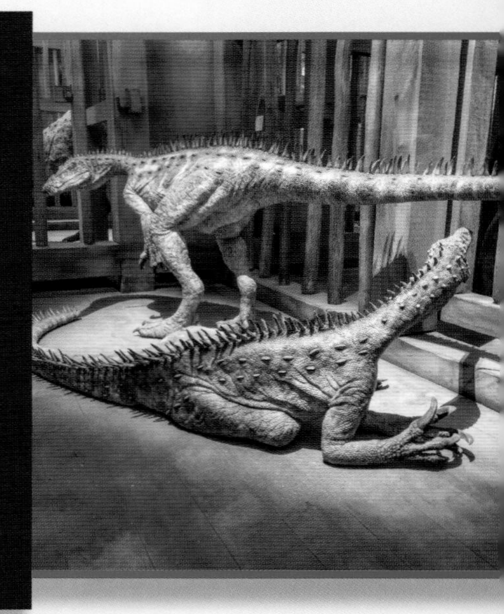

THE TYRANNOSAUR KIND

Status: presumed extinct
Adult lengths: 9–43 ft (2.7–13 m)

REPRESENTATIVE SHOWN: *TYRANNOSAURUS*

- Tyrannosaur tooth marks are routinely identified on apparent prey and healed bite injuries from would-be victims.
- The age of the oldest known tyrannosaur individual is estimated at 28 years.
- The presence of medullary tissues in the bones of a sub-adult *T. rex* indicates that the specimen was female and had reached reproductive maturity before achieving full size.

THE PAKICETID KIND

Status: presumed extinct
Adult lengths: 3.3–6.6 ft (1–2 m)

REPRESENTATIVE SHOWN: *PAKICETUS*

- Recent studies suggest a semi-aquatic lifestyle for pakicetids, but they may have been fully terrestrial.
- They had unusually dense limb bones, possibly to provide ballast in shallow water.
- Pakicetid fossils have been recovered from pre-Ice Age rock layers of India and Pakistan.

What did the Ark's Carnivores eat?

After making everything, the Lord stated that people and animals were to eat vegetation (Genesis 1:29–30). It was not until after the Flood that God permitted man to eat meat (Genesis 9:3). We cannot be sure when certain animals began to eat meat, although the fossil record provides strong evidence that carnivory occurred prior to the Flood.

If carnivorous activity was prevalent in the pre-Flood world, it is still possible that the animals the Lord sent did not eat meat or that they could have survived for one year without it. There have been modern examples of animals normally considered to be carnivores that refused to eat meat, such as the lion known as Little Tyke.

However, if some of the Ark's animals did eat meat, there are several methods of preserving or supplying their food. Meat can be preserved through drying, smoking, salting, or pickling. Certain fish can pack themselves in mud and survive for years without water—these could have been stored on the Ark. Mealworms and other insects can be bred for both carnivores and insectivores.

Do These Look Like Whales?

Pakicetids were a small family of mammals whose remains have been found in Eocene rock layers of Pakistan. Pakicetids are currently promoted in popular models of evolution as transitional forms to ultimately help bridge the gap between extinct land animals and modern whales.

On the one hand, biblical creation does not automatically exclude mode-of-life changes occurring within animal kinds. For instance, we have the example of kakapos—flightless parrots from New Zealand—having apparently descended from flying ancestors. So the basic idea that members of a whale kind shifted from land-dwelling lifestyles to water-dwelling lifestyles may seem somewhat plausible.

On the other hand, one of the greatest weaknesses of the pakicetids-to-whales idea is a lack of evidence. The changes necessary for converting pakicetids into modern whales are extreme and particular; a flood of change contrived from only a few drops of evidence. Even a cursory glance reveals that pakicetids and other supposed whale ancestors were quite unlike modern whales.

THE RHINOCEROS KIND

Status: four living genera
Adult lengths: 5–16 ft (1.5–5 m)

REPRESENTATIVE SHOWN: *TRIGONIAS*

- The earliest known rhinos were relatively small and hornless, or bore small nasal bumps.
- Most members of this kind featured between one and three facial horns.
- Rhinos are unusual in that all living genera are found in rock layers below Ice Age deposits.

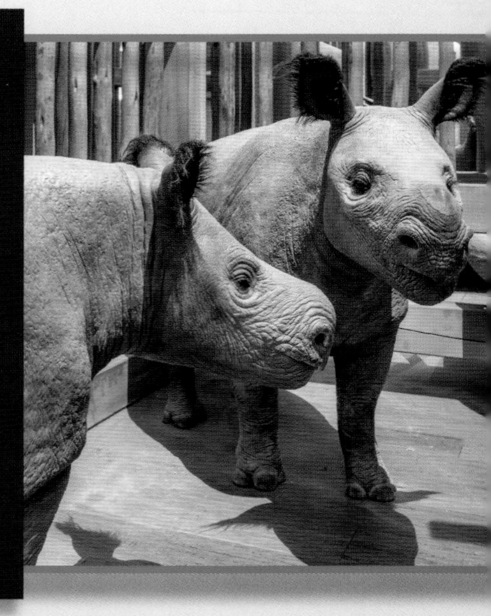

THE CHALICOTHERE KIND

Status: presumed extinct
Adult lengths: 7.5–11 ft (2.3–3.4 m)

REPRESENTATIVE SHOWN: *ANISODON*

- Chalicotheres may have looked a bit like giant ground sloths, but were actually more physically similar to tapirs, rhinos, and horses.
- Minimal tooth wear indicates that these animals ate soft plant material.
- Fossils of this kind persist into the early stages of the Ice Age, though some suggest that the "Nandi bear"—an unconfirmed African animal—may actually be a late-surviving chalicothere.

THE REBBACHISAUR KIND

Status: presumed extinct
Adult lengths: 20–50 ft (6–15 m)

REPRESENTATIVE SHOWN: *NIGERSAURUS*

- Sauropods are known for their great size, but not every variety was extremely massive. Stretching about 15 feet (4.6 m) nose to tail, these young rebbachisaurids are half the size of adults.
- The *Nigersaurus* is named for the Republic of Niger, the nation in which its fossils were originally discovered.
- Facial features indicate that they were low-level grazers, like the behemoth described in Job 40:15–24.

Were Unicorns on the Ark?

Skeptics frequently mock the Bible because some older translations include the word *unicorn* in the text. Naturally, this word conjures up images of a mythical, white horse-like animal with a single horn on its head. But is this what the biblical writers had in mind? Does the Bible mistakenly teach the existence of this mythical animal?

Newer Bible versions translate the Hebrew with terms like "wild ox" or "wild bull." Biblical passages that describe this creature mention the following characteristics:

- Great strength (Numbers 23:22, 24:8)
- Not suitable to keep near children or to use for plowing a field (Job 39:9–10)
- Younger animal can skip about (Psalm 29:6)
- One horn (Psalm 92:10) or two horns (Deuteronomy 33:17)

The characteristics of this creature do not fit the horse or a horse-like animal, but there is an animal that fits these descriptions quite well—the rhinoceros. They are incredibly strong, unfit for domestication, and young rhinos can skip. Rhinos can also have one horn or two horns. And just as is seen on two-horned rhinos today where one horn is larger than the other, Deuteronomy 33:17 mentions the two-horned version of this creature and implies that one horn is larger than the other.

The King James Version of the Bible was translated in 1611. At that time, rhinos were often referred to as unicorns. More than two centuries later, the 1828 edition of Webster's Dictionary included the following definition for unicorn: "An animal with one horn; the Monoceros. The name is often applied to the rhinoceros." This is still reflected in our classification system. The Indian rhinoceros has a single horn and is called *Rhinoceros unicornis*. The black rhinoceros boasts two horns and bears the Latin name *Diceros bicornis*.

Countless skeptics have asked whether there would be unicorns at the Ark Encounter. There is no reason for them to wonder any longer. Here are the Ark's unicorns—the rhinoceros kind.

THE GIRAFFE KIND

Status: two living genera
Adult lengths: 8.2–18 ft (2.5–5.5 m)

REPRESENTATIVE SHOWN: *SHANSITHERIUM*

- The extinct species *Giraffa jumae* was the tallest among known members of the kind, standing about 22 feet (6.7 m) high.
- The skin-covered bony protuberances on giraffid heads—called ossicones—are initially soft and cartilaginous, so as to ease the birthing process.
- These figures are modeled after *Shansitherium*, a medium-sized extinct giraffid from China featuring four ossicones.

THE HORSE KIND

Status: one living genera
Adult lengths: 2.8–12 ft (85 cm–3.8 m)

REPRESENTATIVE SHOWN: *MESOHIPPUS*

- Modern representatives of the horse kind are quite similar overall, but ancient forms were more diverse.
- Members are identified by defining skull and tooth features, and living varieties—horses, donkeys, and zebras—can interbreed.
- The modern-looking genus *Dinohippus* contained both one-toed and three-toed individuals. This is not evolution but variation within the horse kind.

THE HIPPOPOTAMUS KIND

Status: one living genera
Adult lengths: 3.9–14 ft (1.2–4.3 m)

REPRESENTATIVE SHOWN: *CHOEROPSIS*

- Though they have varied in size, and a bit in shape, it seems that hippos have changed relatively little since the Flood.
- Certain extinct varieties (e.g., the giant species, *Hippopotamus gorgops*) featured elevated eye placement, forming low eye stalks on top of their heads.
- Fossils of the living genus *Choeropsis*—also called *Hexaprotodon*—are found in pre-Ice Age rock layers.

WHY IS THE GIRAFFE'S NECK SO SHORT?

Giraffidae is a family of large mammals, currently represented by only two species. They have split hooves and re-chew their food, indicating they qualify as "clean" animals according to the dietary laws described in Leviticus. This means that up to seven pairs of this kind may have boarded the Ark rather than just a single pair.

Today, giraffids are often considered in light of their most popular member: the long-necked giraffe. However, the other living member of the family, the okapi, has more reserved proportions. Indeed, the majority of fossil giraffids had shorter necks than the modern giraffe. This suggests that the Ark giraffids were probably more okapi-like in appearance than the giraffe.

The long neck of the giraffe is only one example of variation within this kind. *Sivatherium,* with its stocky body and branched ossicones, resembled a moose, while *Bramatherium* had a plate of bone on its head that split into four ossicones like an elaborate headdress. Fossil giraffids have been recovered from rock layers as low as the Miocene across Asia, Africa, and Europe.

HOW COULD NOAH FIT ALL THE ANIMALS ON THE ARK?

IMAGINE THE EARTH AS IT WAS BEFORE THE FLOOD.

The forests are lush and fertile. The air is thick, warm, and fragrant. The completed Ark sits quietly on a hilltop like a great wooden fortress.

Guided in pairs, thousands of creatures flood into the Ark. There are perhaps millions of species worldwide, but only select representatives of every land-dependent, air-breathing kind are sent. Approximately 6,744 animals assemble inside—most are small, young, and easily kept. These chosen animals will reestablish their

HOW MANY SPECIES ARE
THERE IN THE WORLD TODAY?

According to estimates published in 2014,* there are fewer than 1.8 million documented species of organisms in the world. Over 98% of these species are fish, invertebrates, and non-animals (like plants and bacteria). This means that there are fewer than 34,000 species of known, land-dependent vertebrates in the world today.

*IUCN 2014. IUCN *Red List of Threatened Species.* Version 2014.3. <www.iucnredlist.org>. Downloaded on 1 July 2016.

THE ARK NEEDED TO HOUSE THE ANCESTORS OF FEWER THAN 34,000 LAND DEPENDENT SPECIES.

WHICH ANIMALS WERE BROUGHT INTO THE ARK?

The Bible says that Noah brought representatives of every land-dependent, air-breathing animal kind. *Kind* is a broader category than *species*, and usually includes many species.

Of flying things after their kind, and of beasts after their kind, of every creeping thing of the earth after his kind, two of every sort shall come unto you, to keep them alive.
(Genesis 6:20)

WHAT IS AN ANIMAL KIND?

An animal kind, or *baramin* (from the Hebrew words for "created" and "kind"), is a group of related animals not related to any other animals. The study of created kinds is called baraminology.

HOW MANY KINDS WERE ON THE ARK?

Studies beginning in 2012 estimate that among land-dependent vertebrates, there are fewer than 1,400 known living and extinct kinds. In a worst-case scenario, it is projected that Noah was responsible for fewer than 6,744 individual animals—most of them small and easily maintained.

OBSERVABLE PROCESSES SHOW SPECIATION WITHIN KINDS, NOT EVOLUTION OF ONE KIND INTO ANOTHER KIND

NATURAL SELECTION

Natural selection is an observable process in which creatures possessing specific traits survive better than others in a given environment. While commonly promoted as a driving force of molecules-to-man evolution, natural selection cannot bring about the changes required to turn one kind of creature into another. Natural selection is only able to act on pre-existing features, and contrary to popular belief, it cannot create new ones.

MUTATIONS

A mutation is essentially a permanent change to the DNA of an organism. Evolutionists consider random mutations to be the primary means of producing new genetic information. However, the vast majority of observed mutations have negative effects, and the mutations that are either "neutral" or somehow beneficial still do not add the information necessary to transform one kind of organism into a totally different kind, such as dinosaurs evolving into birds.

OTHER MECHANISMS

Other mechanisms are often cited that supposedly contribute to the evolutionary process, such as sexual selection, founder effect, and genetic drift. No one has demonstrated that these are capable of producing the vast amount of new genetic information required to change one kind of creature into a completely different kind.

HOW COULD SO FEW KINDS BECOME SO MANY SPECIES?

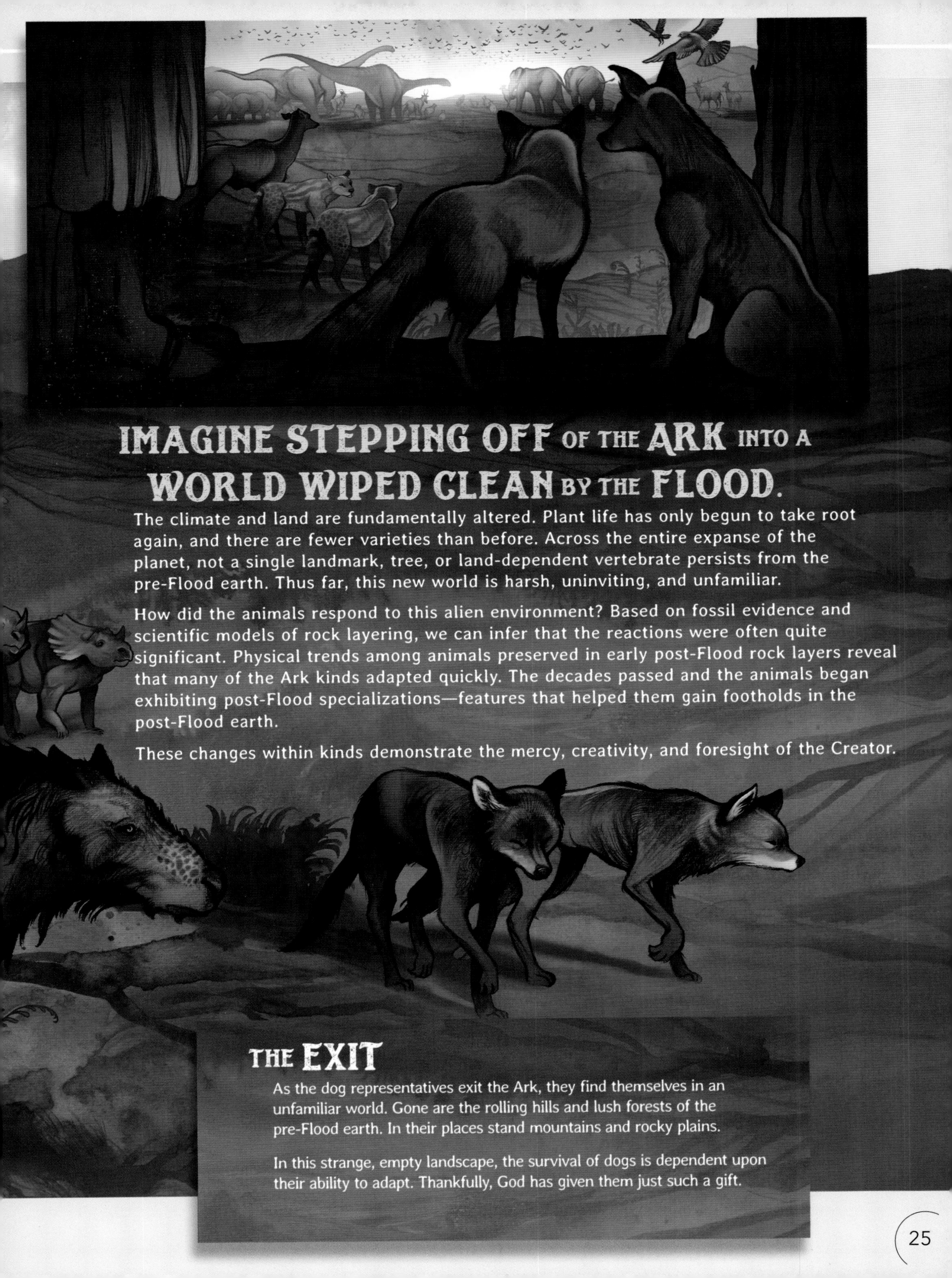

IMAGINE STEPPING OFF OF THE ARK INTO A WORLD WIPED CLEAN BY THE FLOOD.

The climate and land are fundamentally altered. Plant life has only begun to take root again, and there are fewer varieties than before. Across the entire expanse of the planet, not a single landmark, tree, or land-dependent vertebrate persists from the pre-Flood earth. Thus far, this new world is harsh, uninviting, and unfamiliar.

How did the animals respond to this alien environment? Based on fossil evidence and scientific models of rock layering, we can infer that the reactions were often quite significant. Physical trends among animals preserved in early post-Flood rock layers reveal that many of the Ark kinds adapted quickly. The decades passed and the animals began exhibiting post-Flood specializations—features that helped them gain footholds in the post-Flood earth.

These changes within kinds demonstrate the mercy, creativity, and foresight of the Creator.

THE EXIT

As the dog representatives exit the Ark, they find themselves in an unfamiliar world. Gone are the rolling hills and lush forests of the pre-Flood earth. In their places stand mountains and rocky plains.

In this strange, empty landscape, the survival of dogs is dependent upon their ability to adapt. Thankfully, God has given them just such a gift.

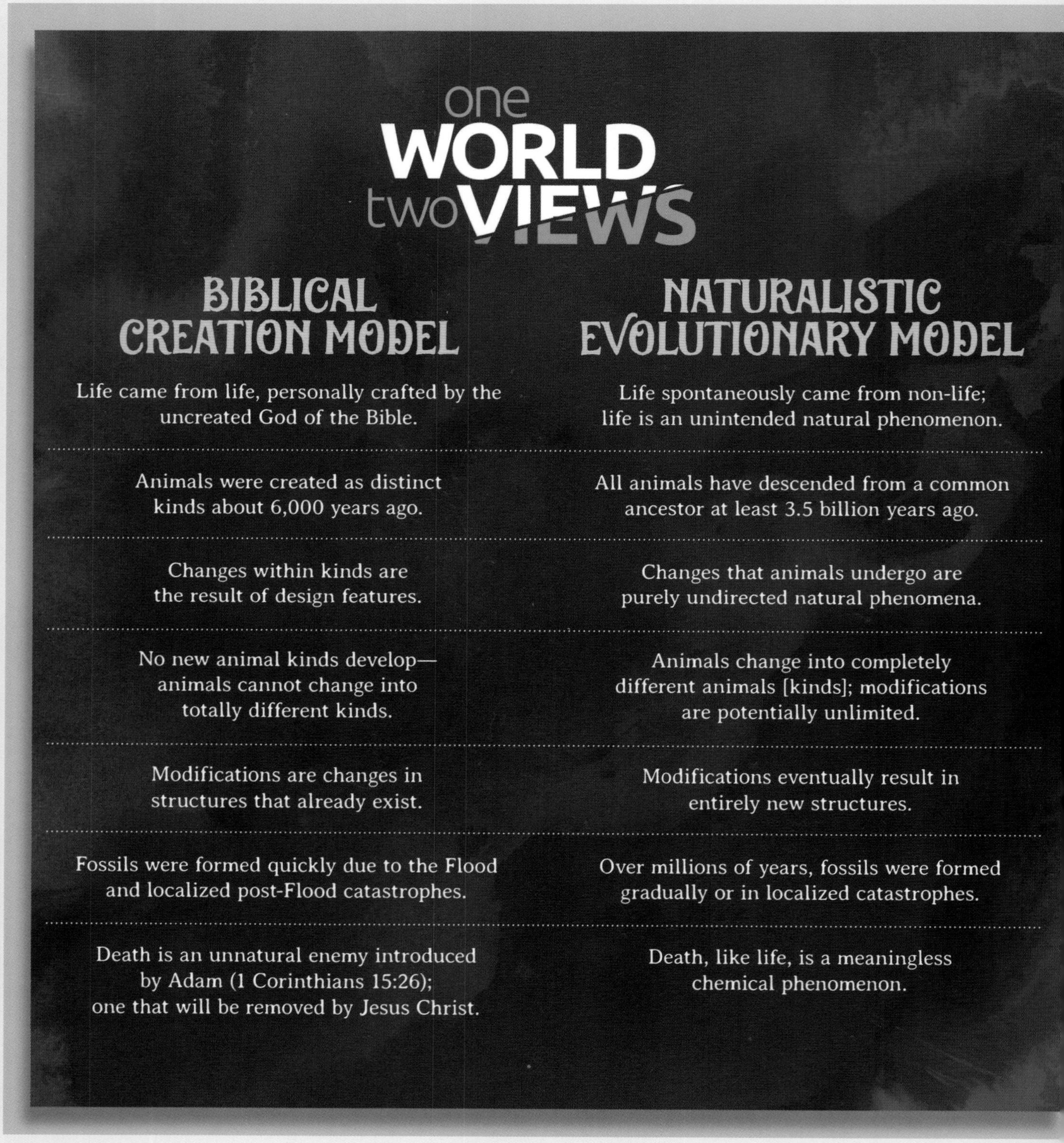

one WORLD two VIEWS

BIBLICAL CREATION MODEL	NATURALISTIC EVOLUTIONARY MODEL
Life came from life, personally crafted by the uncreated God of the Bible.	Life spontaneously came from non-life; life is an unintended natural phenomenon.
Animals were created as distinct kinds about 6,000 years ago.	All animals have descended from a common ancestor at least 3.5 billion years ago.
Changes within kinds are the result of design features.	Changes that animals undergo are purely undirected natural phenomena.
No new animal kinds develop—animals cannot change into totally different kinds.	Animals change into completely different animals [kinds]; modifications are potentially unlimited.
Modifications are changes in structures that already exist.	Modifications eventually result in entirely new structures.
Fossils were formed quickly due to the Flood and localized post-Flood catastrophes.	Over millions of years, fossils were formed gradually or in localized catastrophes.
Death is an unnatural enemy introduced by Adam (1 Corinthians 15:26); one that will be removed by Jesus Christ.	Death, like life, is a meaningless chemical phenomenon.

EVOLUTIONARY SHORTCOMINGS

LIFE FROM NON-LIFE

Naturalistic forms of evolution have fatal flaws, including their inability to explain the origin of life. The idea that life spontaneously formed from non-living matter through chance chemical reactions has never been observed in nature or replicated in the lab. Even if scientists were someday able to create life in a laboratory, it would demonstrate that the creation of life requires great intelligence. The Law of Biogenesis explains that life only comes from living organisms.

IS ANYBODY OUT THERE?

To avoid the impossibility of life forming from non-life, some individuals, including prominent scientists, promote an idea called panspermia—that life on earth had its origins elsewhere in the universe.

This alien proposal "passes the buck" on the original problem. If life could not evolve from non-life on earth, a planet perfectly suited for life, why should we assume that life could evolve from non-life elsewhere? This view attaches the additional difficulty of safely transporting life to earth.

LIVING IN A MATERIAL WORLD

A huge problem for naturalistic thinking is its foundation in materialism—the belief that only matter exists. However, morality, laws of logic, and laws of nature are all non-physical. For example, no one can swing by a grocery store and buy two ounces of logic, a bag of natural law, and a carton of morality. In a universe without laws of logic or laws of nature, how could anyone prove that naturalistic evolution has occurred? Indeed, how could anyone know anything at all if our thoughts are merely chemical reactions?

THE WORST OF BOTH WORLDS

Some people attempt to combine aspects of biblical creation with evolution/millions of years. This idea contradicts the Bible at numerous points, including the following:

- Death entered the world when Adam sinned (Romans 5:12, 8:20–22)
- Thorns and thistles originated with the Curse (Genesis 3:18)
- Man and woman were created at the beginning of history (Mark 10:6)

Each of these details are necessarily denied by "old-earth" perspectives and end up undermining the truth of Scripture. If we cannot believe God concerning how He made the universe, then why should we believe Him about the salvation offered through Jesus Christ?

ANIMAL CARE

HOW COULD NOAH'S FAMILY TEND THOUSANDS OF ANIMALS?

MANAGEABLE WORKLOADS

God commanded Noah to bring representatives of every land-dependent kind of animal on the Ark. Providing for such a diverse assembly of creatures would have involved a lot of work. Based on our calculations, each family member would have been responsible for an average of about 850 animals.

WORKABLE MODELS

Have you ever wondered how Noah's family fed all the animals and removed their waste? How did they provide fresh air and water? And how did they light the Ark? The concepts displayed in this exhibit are models showing plausible solutions to these challenges.

While we may not know all of the details, we know they successfully accomplished their tasks since all eight people and the animals God sent to them survived the Flood (Genesis 8:15–19).

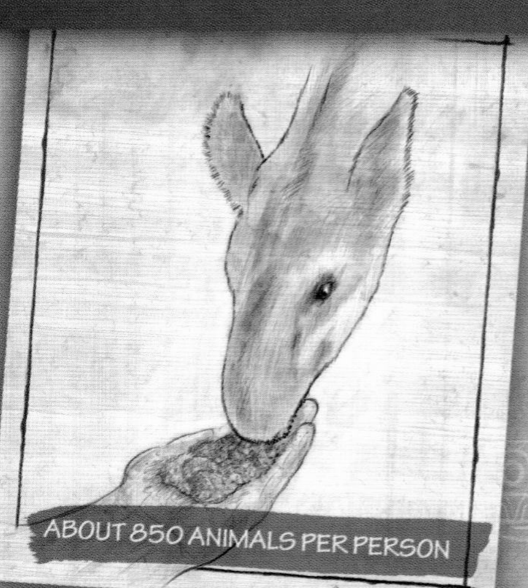

ABOUT 850 ANIMALS PER PERSON

SMALL ANIMALS

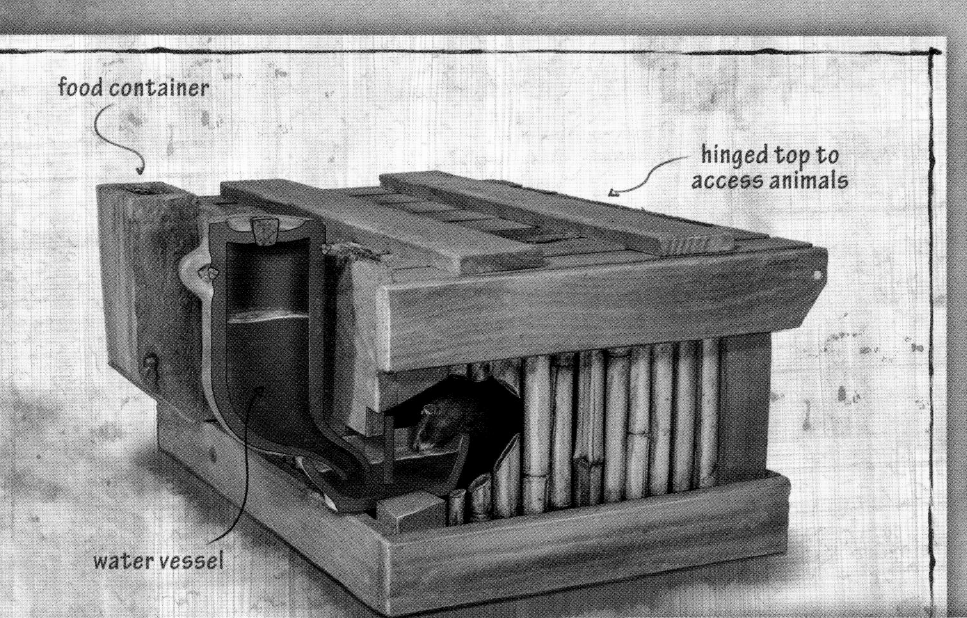

SMART FEEDERS

Noah's family may have used automated processes to handle many of the responsibilities related to animal care. Food and water systems could have been used to contain several days' worth of nourishment, allowing creatures to eat and drink whenever they wanted.

DROPPINGS

Slotted floors in the cages combined with a series of angled trays placed beneath them would move the waste of many animals to a collection tray at the bottom of the stack that could be quickly cleaned.

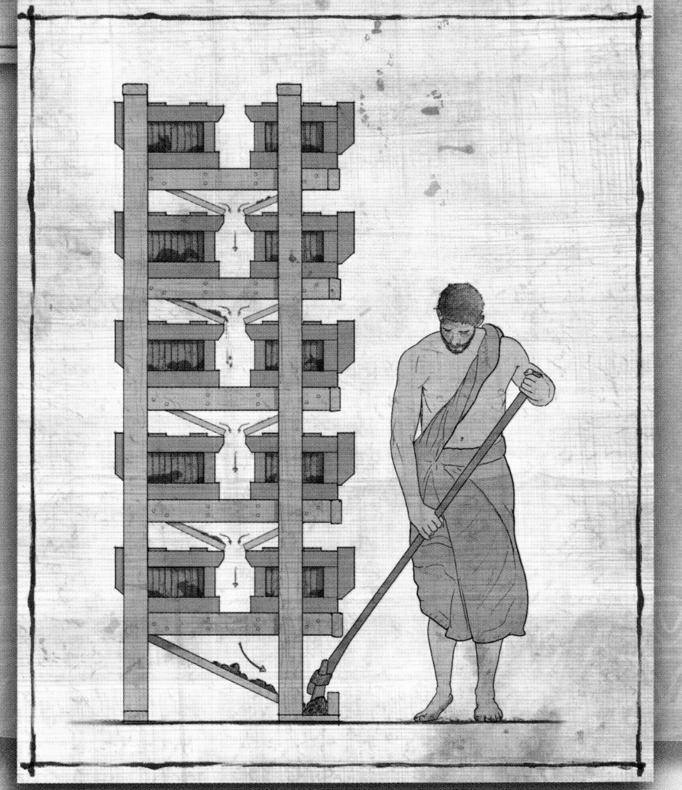

LARGE ANIMALS

WATER DISTRIBUTION

Water collected from the roof may have been stored in cisterns and then transferred through bamboo piping to smaller tanks. Valves and spigots could be used to control water flow into and out of these large clay vessels near the animal enclosures.

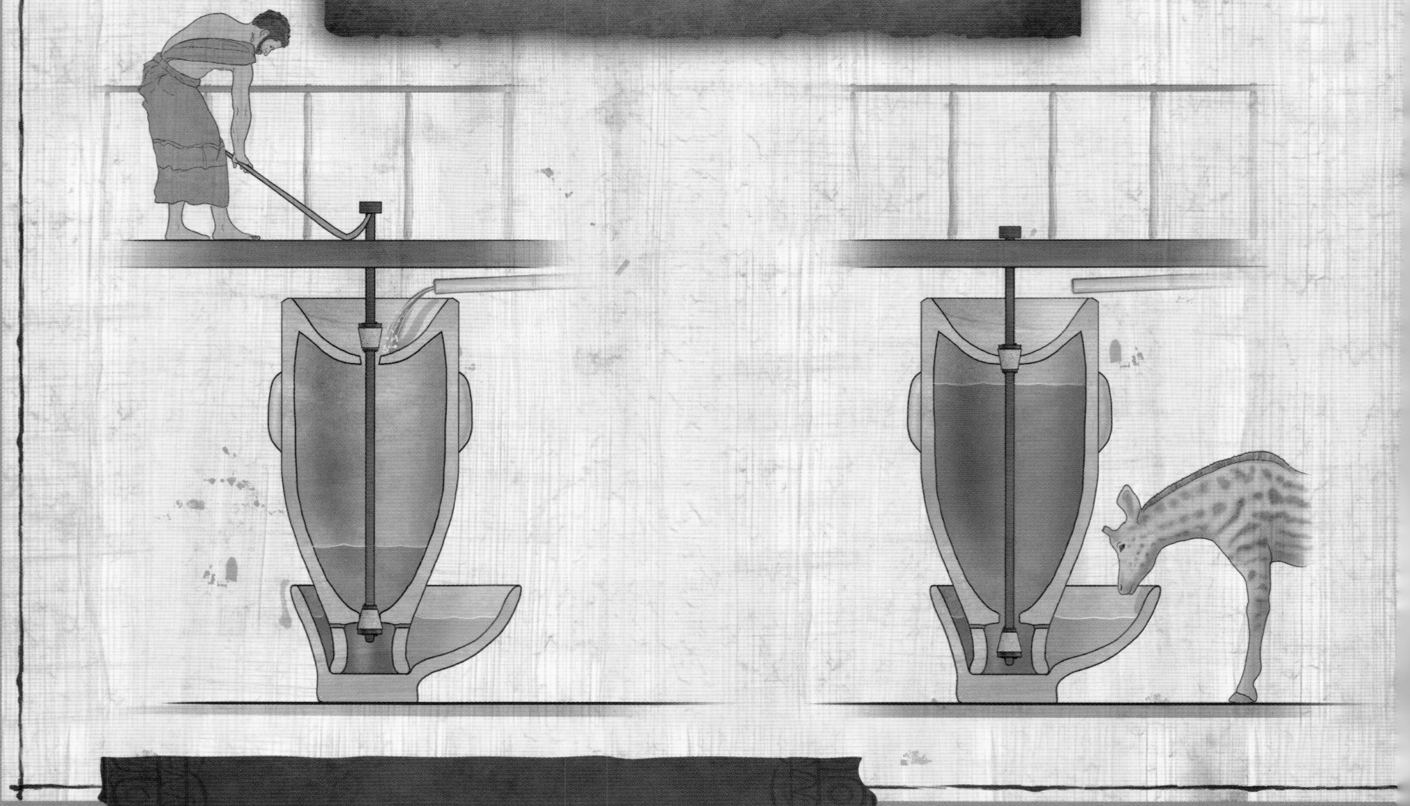

WASTE REMOVAL

Large animals would have produced plenty of waste during the Flood. Liquid waste could be drained away by a gutter system leading to an Ark-wide liquid waste collection. Solid waste could be moved to a solid waste collection area with shovels and wheelbarrows.

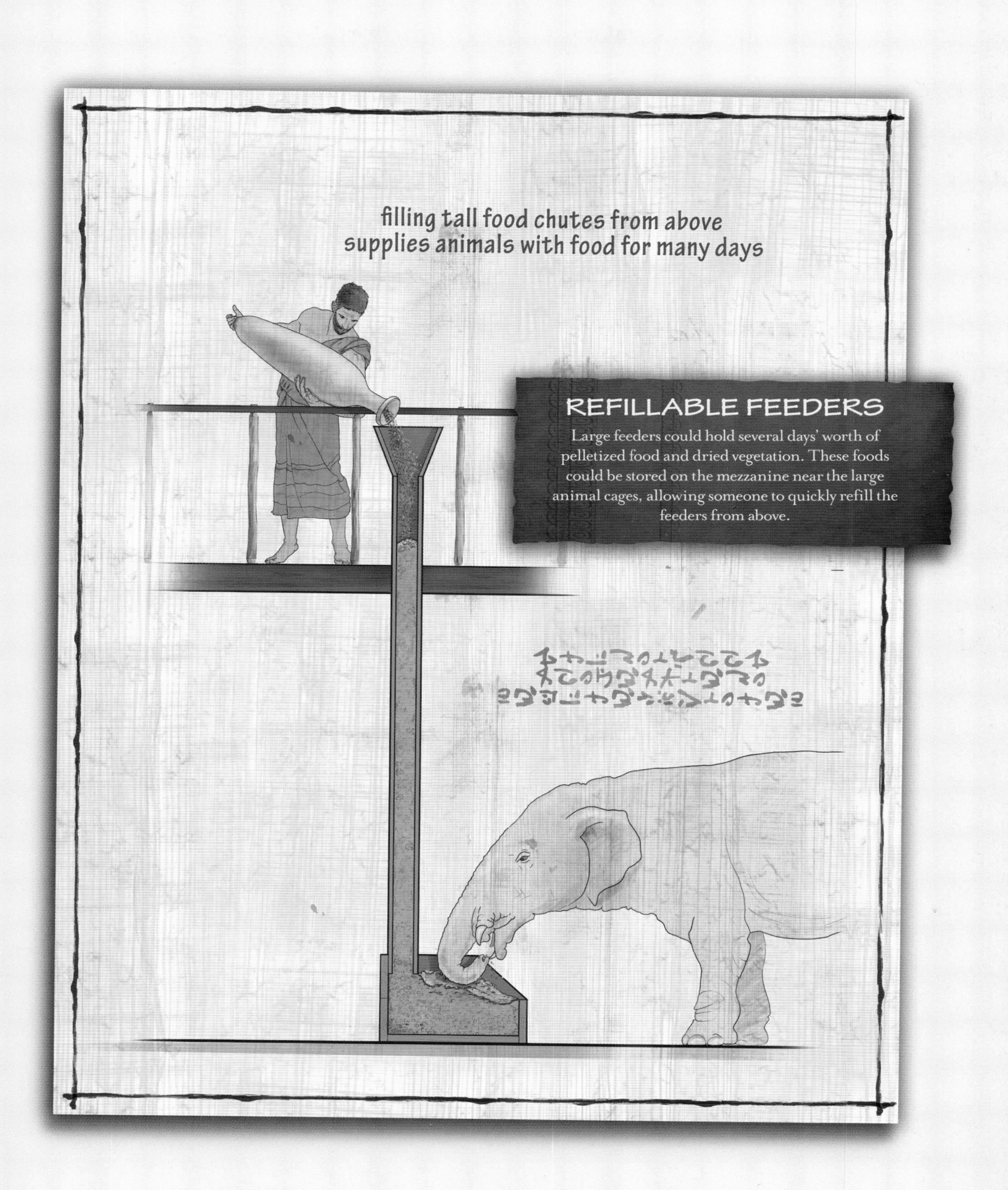
filling tall food chutes from above
supplies animals with food for many days
REFILLABLE FEEDERS
Large feeders could hold several days' worth of pelletized food and dried vegetation. These foods could be stored on the mezzanine near the large animal cages, allowing someone to quickly refill the feeders from above.

REPTILES AND AMPHIBIANS

SLIMY SOLUTIONS

Providing for hundreds of reptiles and amphibians would present unique challenges. The smaller varieties could have been kept in clay pots with some water at the bottom, allowing these animals to be kept in moist environments, if necessary. Fresh water could be poured through the pot's fabric coverings and waste removed through a drainage system.

MULTIPLYING MOTHS

If the animals ate insects, a series of moth cribs would allow moths to climb directly into the pots, providing a renewable food source for the reptiles and amphibians.

PICKY EATERS

SPECIALIZED DIETS

How could Noah's family provide the proper food for animals with unique diets? For example, vampire bats drink blood, anteaters eat ants, and koalas survive almost exclusively on leaves of the eucalyptus tree. While it may have been possible for Noah's family to provide these specific foods, it is unlikely they would need to.

KOALAS

Koalas can eat the leaves of some other trees, such as the wattle, paperbark, and tea trees, but they prefer certain eucalyptus leaves. Like other animals, the koala's Ark ancestors were less specialized, and probably heartier than modern representatives. As such, they may have eaten a much wider variety of food, including grains, fruits, and vegetables.

VAMPIRE BATS

The bat exhibit on the first deck mentioned that every bat may have derived from a single kind. Modern varieties of these animals, such as the vampire bat, have become more specialized over time. In fact, the vampire bat is part of a family that includes fruit eaters and insect eaters. So the Ark ancestors of these creatures did not need to survive on a blood diet.

ANTEATERS

As their name suggests, anteaters thrive on eating ants and can devour up to 35,000 insects a day. However, anteaters in captivity are often fed fruit and eggs. In the wild, giant anteaters also consume fruit that has dropped to the ground while the other anteater species can climb trees to get fruit.

VENTILATION

POSSIBLE AIR-FRESHENING TECHNIQUES

MOON POOL CONCEPT

1. Falling waves inside the moon pool pull in fresh air.
2. Rising waves push the fresh air through the shaft to the bottom deck.
3. Fresh air is directed into the lower level, ultimately bringing air to the other decks.

WAVE-POWERED PURIFIER

Moon pools are generally used for drilling and research vessels, but the same concept could be applied to exploit the waves to pump air throughout the Ark. It may seem strange to include a shaft or well inside of the Ark that opens to the water below, but a moon pool would be an extremely effective mechanism to provide a continual supply of fresh air.

CONVECTION

Many modern buildings that house large numbers of animals do not require any special mechanical system for ventilation. Instead, they rely on the natural convection currents to circulate air. In addition to the possible opening along the roof, sufficient air flow could be produced by the temperature difference between cool surfaces in the Ark and the body heat generated by warm-blooded animals.

OTHER POTENTIAL METHODS

The Ark may have included a variety of ingenious methods to circulate air. A furnace fueled by animal waste could have been used to heat air and create a draft in a specially constructed flue and chimney system. Another possibility is that people or animals powered mechanical bellows or fans that could have been built to blow air through the Ark.

LIGHTING

POSSIBLE WAYS TO LIGHT A DARK ARK

ARTIFICIAL LIGHTING

Artificial lighting may have been used throughout the Ark. Olive oil could have been used as a long-lasting fuel source for lamps lighting the dark interior. Although not necessarily as safe of an option as an oil lamp, other open flame sources, such as candles or torches could have been employed.

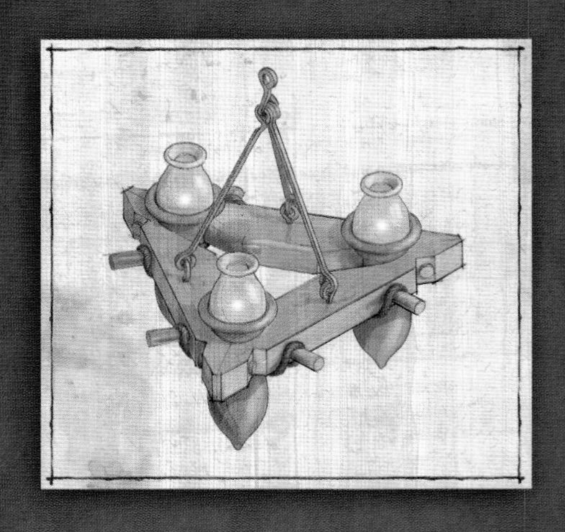

SUNLIGHT THROUGH "OPENING"

The Lord instructed Noah to make the Ark's roof and to finish it "to a cubit from the top" (Genesis 6:16). Some translations mention a window in this context, but the normal Hebrew word for window is not used. This phrase may refer to a cubit-high opening under the roof. If this is accurate, light could have spilled through this opening to light the Ark.

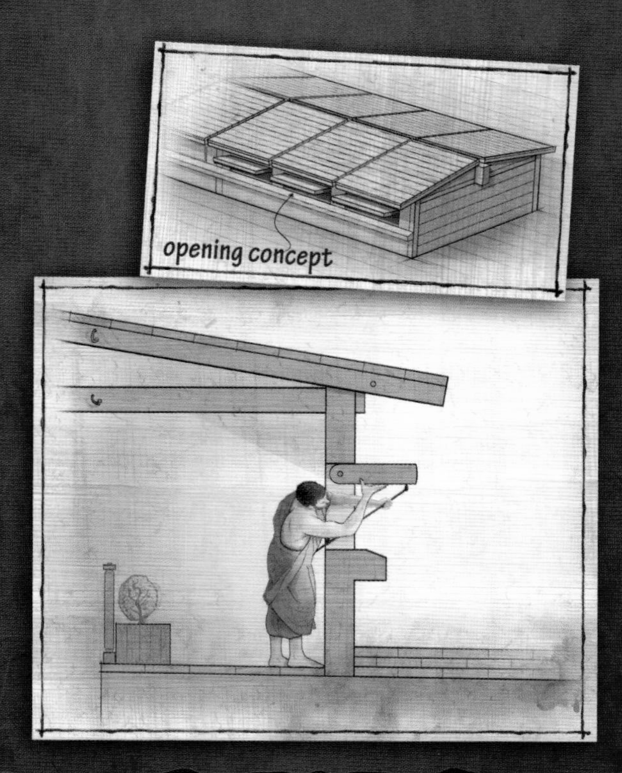

SUNLIGHT THROUGH "COVERING"

Genesis 8:13 states that Noah removed the Ark's covering as the earth dried near the end of their time on the Ark. The word used for covering refers to something other than the window Noah used for the birds and "the opening" depicted in the adjacent illustration. The covering may have been a section of the roof that could be drawn back to serve as a central skylight.

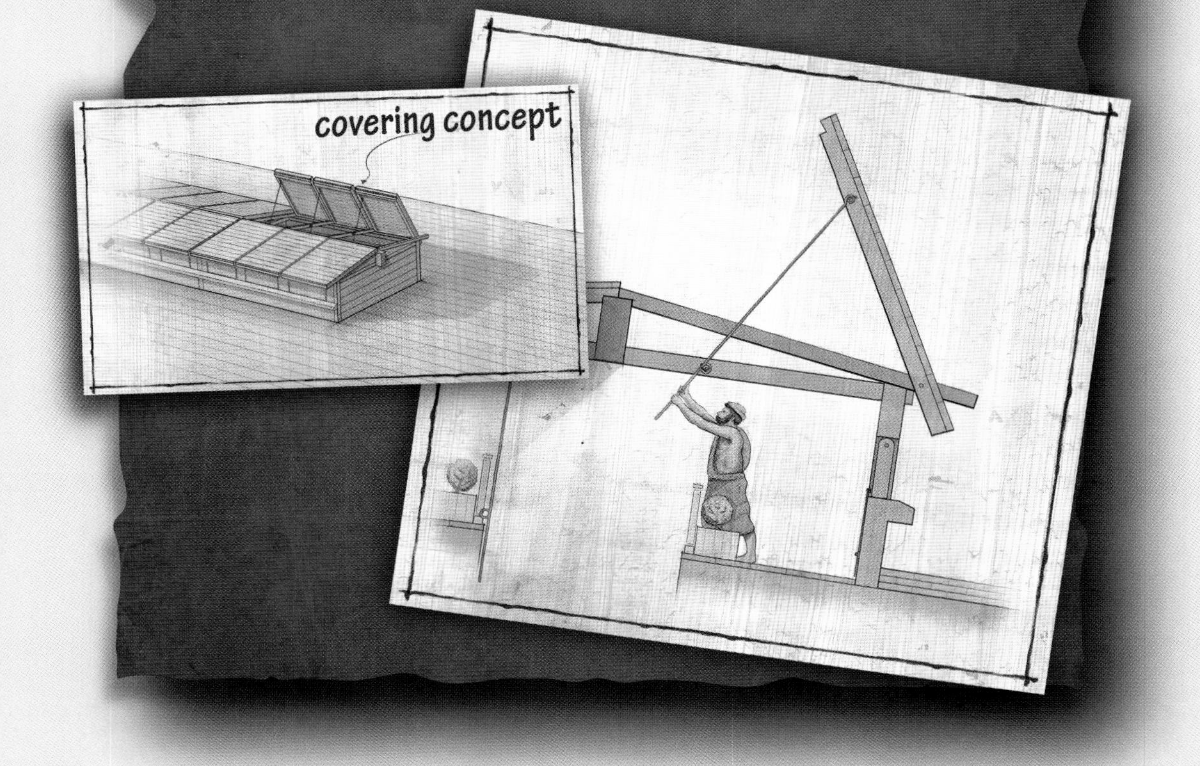

WATER AND WASTE

POSSIBLE LABOR-SAVING SYSTEMS ON THE ARK

CLEAN WATER

To provide fresh water on the Ark, rainwater collected from the roof could be funneled to large, strategically placed storage tanks. A system of spigots and bamboo, or even copper pipes could have delivered water throughout the Ark.

Did you know? Due to the surface area of the Ark's roof, one inch of rainfall per week would have kept cisterns full.

LIQUID WASTE REMOVAL

The large animal cages could have been connected to a valved drainage system, which would prevent backflow and channel urine into a central liquid waste container spanning all three decks. There are at least two ways the liquid waste could have been lifted and dumped into the sea through the vertical shaft.

First, a bucket system powered by the animal treadmill could scoop and dump the waste. The second option would use high pressure created by waves in the moon pool to force the liquid waste through a pipe and dump it into the sea.

SOLID WASTE REMOVAL

After mucking large animal stalls and scraping droppings from the small animal collection troughs, solid waste could have been placed into wheelbarrows and moved to a vertical conveyer system. Powered by an animal on a treadmill, this device would dump the waste into a vertical shaft that opened to the sea.

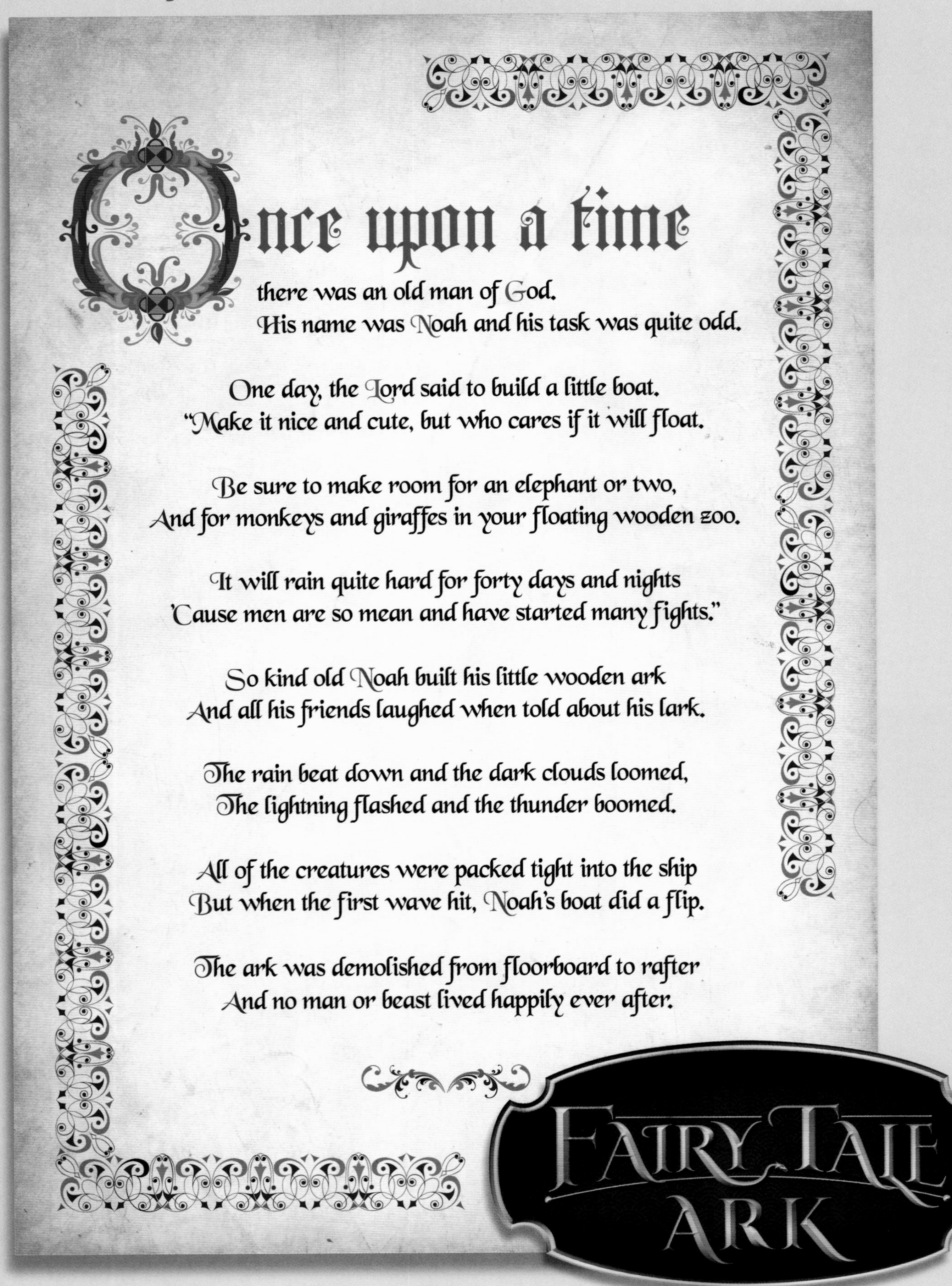
Once upon a time
there was an old man of God.
His name was Noah and his task was quite odd.
One day, the Lord said to build a little boat.
"Make it nice and cute, but who cares if it will float.
Be sure to make room for an elephant or two,
And for monkeys and giraffes in your floating wooden zoo.
It will rain quite hard for forty days and nights
'Cause men are so mean and have started many fights."
So kind old Noah built his little wooden ark
And all his friends laughed when told about his lark.
The rain beat down and the dark clouds loomed,
The lightning flashed and the thunder boomed.
All of the creatures were packed tight into the ship
But when the first wave hit, Noah's boat did a flip.
The ark was demolished from floorboard to rafter
And no man or beast lived happily ever after.
FAIRY TALE
ARK

IF I CAN CONVINCE YOU
THAT THE FLOOD WAS NOT REAL,
THEN I CAN CONVINCE YOU THAT
HEAVEN AND HELL
ARE NOT REAL.

7 D's of Deception

The Bible explains that the size of the Ark was 300 x 50 x 30 cubits. Using artistic license and stylizing the Ark is not necessarily sinful, but these cute arks drastically distort Scripture and make the account look like a fairy tale.

Disregarding God's Word

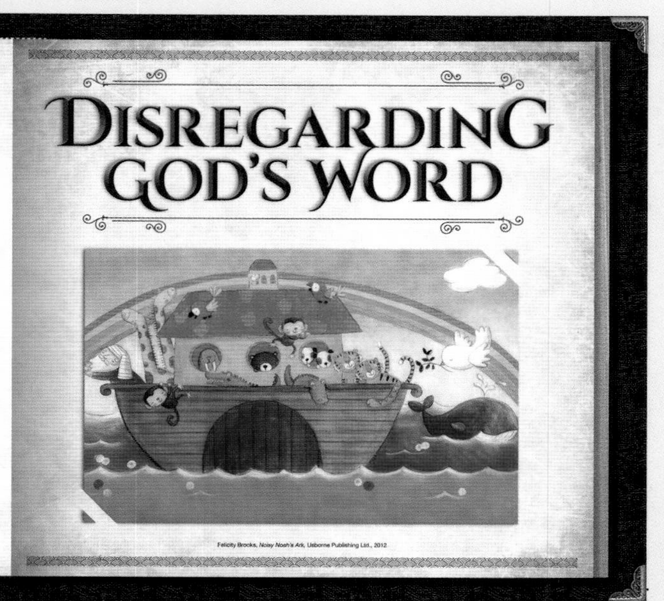

Felicity Brooks, *Noisy Noah's Ark*, Usborne Publishing Ltd., 2012

7 D's of Deception

Fairy tale ark stories often focus on cute animals on a fun boat ride. But the Flood account is about the righteous and holy God judging an exceedingly sinful world with a cataclysmic Flood while showing mercy to Noah's family and the animals.

Distorting the Message

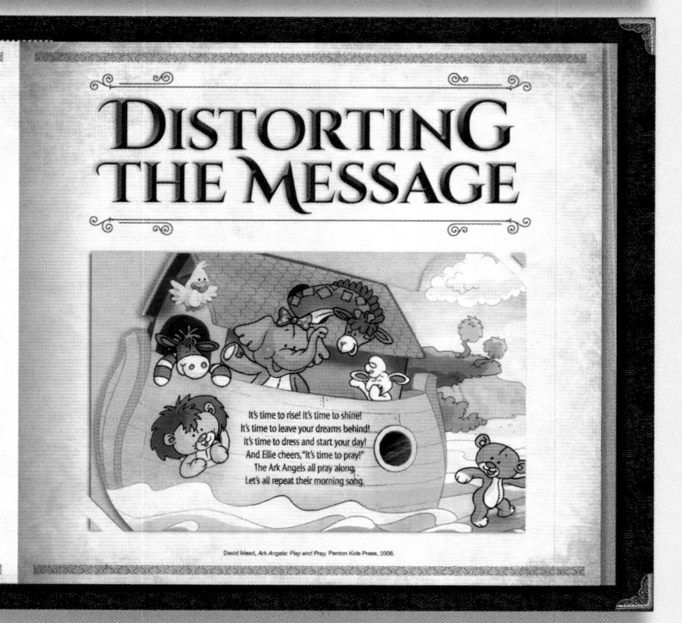

It's time to rise! It's time to shine!
It's time to leave your dreams behind!
It's time to dress and start your day!
And Ellie cheers, "It's time to pray!"
The Ark Angels all pray along.
Let's all repeat their morning song.

David Mead, *Ark Angels: Play and Pray*, Penton Kids Press, 2006.

7D's of Deception

Many of the fairy tale arks are extremely cute and were surely drawn with great intentions.

However, cute things are not necessarily innocent or harmless, and good intentions can lead to disastrous consequences.

Deceptively Cute

Fiona Boon, *My Very First Bible*, Make Believe Ideas Ltd., 2012

7D's of Deception

Many atheists and other skeptics love to use fairy tale arks to mock the Bible. Christians should be defending the truth of God's Word against skeptical attacks rather than providing ammunition to enemies of our Lord.

Discrediting the Truth

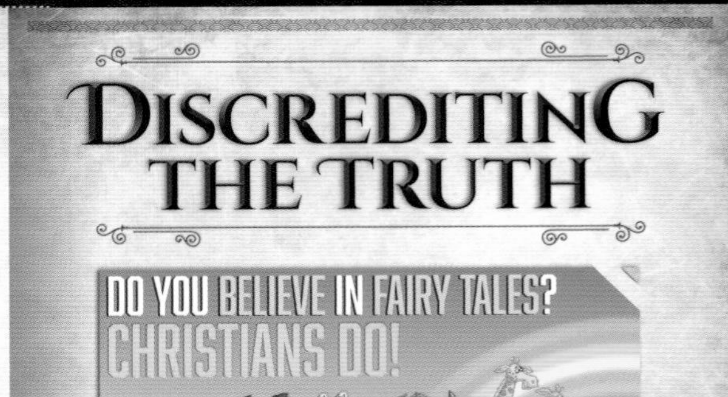

This image is representative of numerous cartoons developed by skeptics using a fairy tale ark to mock the Bible.

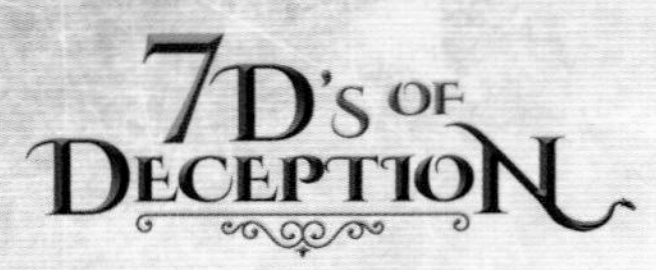

The cute fairy tale arks are not only marketed to children; thousands of items featuring whimsical arks have been made for adults too. The abundance of these fanciful objects attacks the truthfulness of Scripture.

Destructive for All Ages

Franklin Mint Heirloom Recommendation, *Two By Two*, 1991

7 D's of Deception

Some children's books send mixed messages by citing the biblical dimensions of the Ark while displaying an image of a fairy tale ark. Presenting contradictory information confuses readers rather than properly instructing them.

Disorienting the Reader

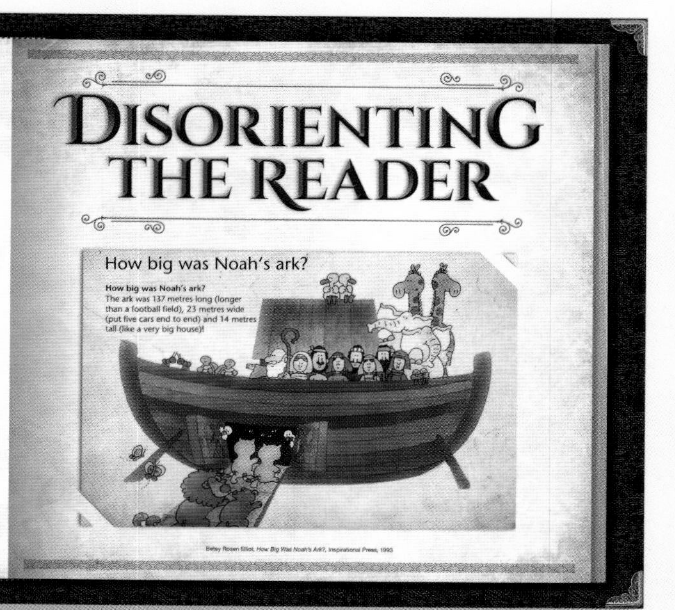

Betsy Rosen Elliot, *How Big Was Noah's Ark?*, Inspirational Press, 1993

7 D's of Deception

By treating Noah's Ark and the Flood as fairy tales rather than sobering reminders of divine judgment on a sin-filled world, these storybooks frequently trivialize the Lord's righteous and holy character.

Defaming God's Character

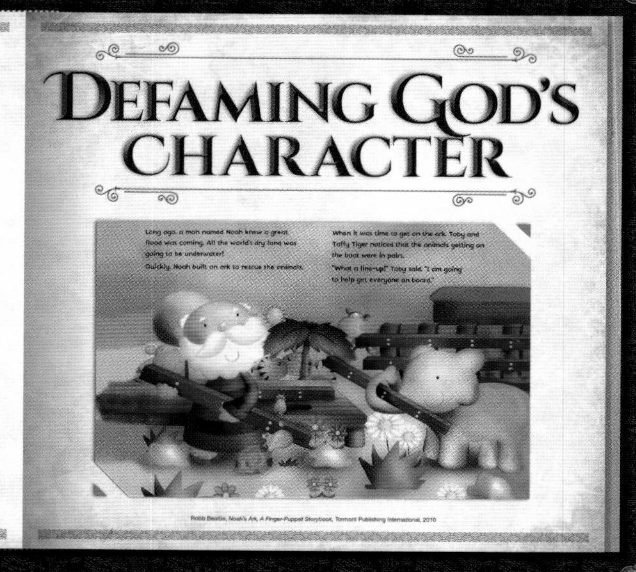

Robb Beattie, *Noah's Ark, A Finger-Puppet Storybook*, Tormont Publishing International, 2010

And everyone died except the 8 people in the Ark.

Genesis 7:23

WHY IS DEATH THE PUNISHMENT FOR SIN ?

Death might seem like a harsh consequence for sin,[1] but we fail to understand the wretchedness of sin compared to God's holiness. God is entirely pure and set apart from evil, and in His perfect justice He must punish sin.

Also, in one sense, death is a merciful punishment. Can you imagine what it would be like to live forever in a fallen world? Wicked people would never die, and if they knew there were no serious consequences for sin, then they would act however they wanted, and the world would become even worse.

[1] Romans 6:23
For the wages of sin is death, but the gift of God is eternal life in Christ Jesus our Lord.

Struggling to come to grips with the reality that everyone outside the Ark died in the Flood, Japheth's wife, Rayneh, ponders sincere questions many people wrestle with today.

IS GOD CRUEL?

There is no question that a great deal of evil and suffering is in the world, which often leads people to wonder whether a loving God exists. The Bible gives us the correct perspective for understanding why there is so much death and suffering.

In the beginning, God created a perfect world and gave man authority over it. Our first parents, Adam and Eve, rejected all that God had offered them and chose to rebel, even though they knew the consequence was death.[1] Death, suffering, violence, and disease are in our world because of what man has done in committing high treason against our holy God.

[1] Genesis 2:16–17
You may freely eat from every tree of the garden, but you must not eat from the tree of the knowledge of good and evil. In the day that you eat of it, you will surely die.

WAS IT **JUST** FOR GOD TO **JUDGE** THE WHOLE WORLD?

First, God created all living things, which gives Him authority over them. Since He is the one who gave life, He has the right to take life. Second, God is perfectly just and must judge sin. Third, all have sinned and deserve death and judgment.[1]

The fact that God allows us to live at all demonstrates His abundant mercy. And as if that were not enough, He has provided the way for man to be saved from sin and dwell eternally with Him through the sacrificial death and Resurrection of His Son, Jesus Christ.[2]

[1] Romans 3:23
For all have sinned and fall short of the glory of God.

[2] Romans 10:9
If you confess with your mouth, "Jesus is Lord," and believe in your heart that God raised Him from the dead, you will be saved.

WHY DOES A **LOVING GOD** ALLOW SO MUCH **DEATH & SUFFERING** ?

If the God of the Bible is truly all-powerful and loving, why has He not put an end to death and suffering? Is He incapable or unwilling to do it?

The Bible states that one day death and suffering will be no more. Right now, God is patiently delaying the final judgment to give people time to turn to Him.[1]

We need to understand that as sinners, we all deserve to die. However, through Jesus Christ, God has provided the way for us to spend eternity with Him in a place where there is no suffering, sorrow, or pain.[2] Death will finally die.[3]

[1] 2 Peter 3:9
The Lord is not slow to fulfill His promise…He is patient toward you, not wishing for any to perish but for all to come to repentance.

[2] Revelation 21:3–4
They will be His people, and God Himself will be with them. God will wipe away every tear from their eyes. There will be no more death. Grief, crying, and pain will no longer exist, because the former things have passed away.

[3] 1 Corinthians 15:26
The last enemy to be destroyed is death.

THE DOOR

"I am the door. Whoever enters through Me will be saved." (John 10:9)

When God told Noah to build the Ark to survive the Flood He would send upon an exceedingly wicked world, He instructed Noah to put one door in the side of the Ark.

"...and put the door of the Ark in its side." (Genesis 6:16)

Noah and his family entered the Ark through that one door to be saved from the watery judgment.

"Enter the Ark, you and your whole family, for I have found you righteous before Me in this generation... So Noah and his sons and his wife and his sons' wives went into the Ark because of the waters of the Flood." (Genesis 7:1, 7)

Noah and his family entering the Ark through the door reminds us of the good news of Jesus Christ.

JESUS IS OUR **ONE DOOR** TO SALVATION

Just as God judged the world with the Flood, He will judge it again, but the final judgment will be by fire. We have all sinned against our holy Creator and deserve the penalty of death. Unless God forgives us of our sins, when we die we would be separated from Him forever in what the Bible calls the second death (Revelation 20:14).

However, God has provided the means of salvation for us by sending His Son, Jesus Christ, to die as our substitute on the Cross. Jesus endured the penalty for our sin and conquered death by rising from the grave. Everyone who asks for His forgiveness and trusts in Him will be saved from the second death and live with Him for eternity.

"I am the way, the truth, and the life. No one comes to the Father except through Me." (John 14:6)

The Ark's door reminds us that we need to go through a door to be saved. Jesus Christ is our one door to salvation, the "Ark" that saves us from God's judgment for eternity.

THE FLOOD BEGINS

On the 17th day of the second month of Noah's 600th year all the waters of the great deep and all the waters from the sky let loose upon the earth. Great fissures form in the earth's crust.

A NEW WORLD

In approximately one year, the wicked pre-Flood world consisting of a supercontinent is destroyed and a new world with seven continents rises from the waters. They are covered with layers of fossil-filled sediment deposited by water, testifying of the biblical account in Genesis. Noah's family is given an opportunity to start over—to be fruitful, multiply, and fill the earth.

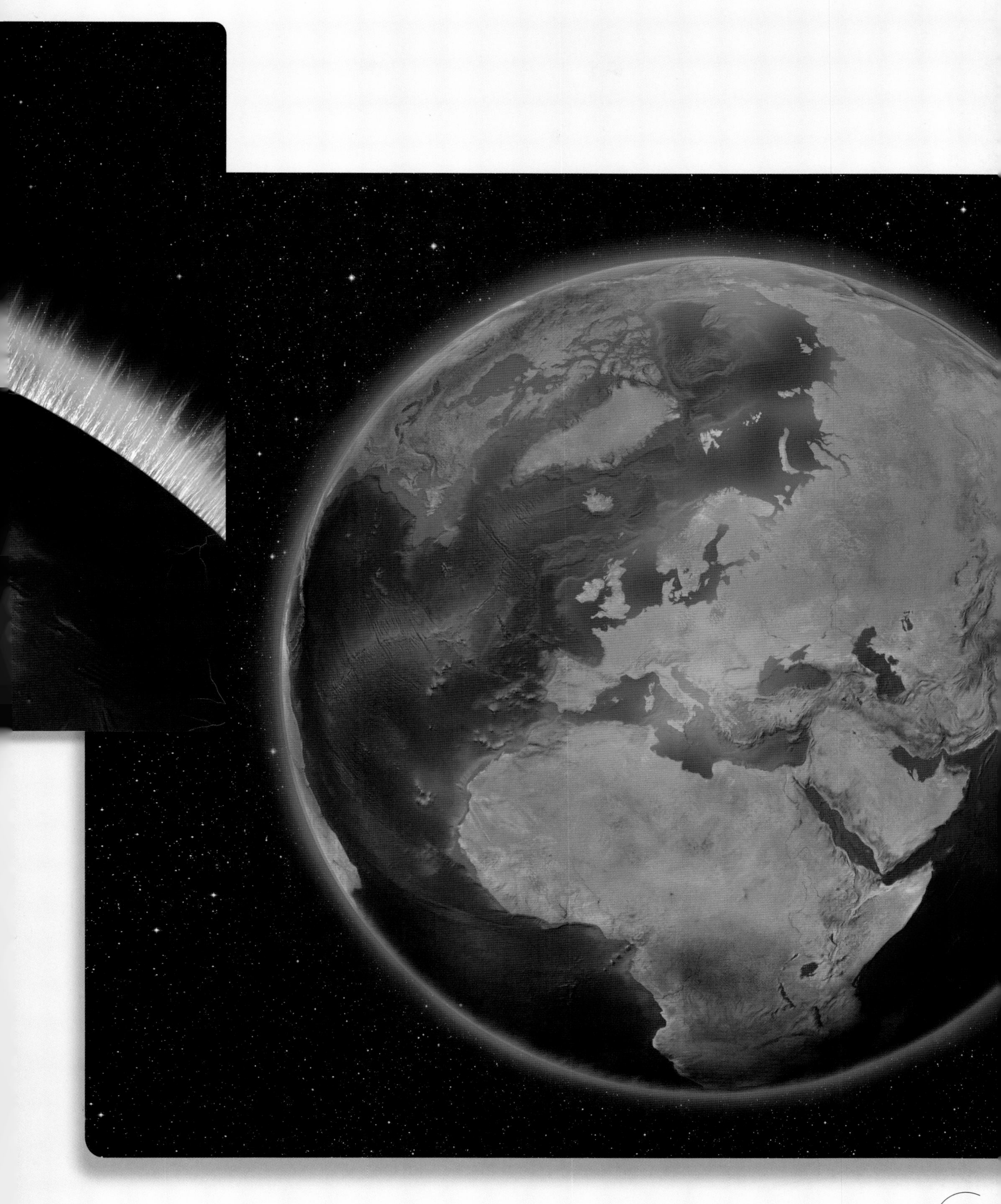

FISSURES WIDEN IN EARTH'S CRUST

As fissures widen in the earth's crust magma comes into contact with seawater, creating massive steam jets. These steam jets shoot through the ocean and into the upper atmosphere generating intensely heavy global rainfall for 40 days and nights.

WATER LEVELS RISE GLOBALLY

Tsunamis batter the fragments of the earth's original supercontinent which are by now quickly moving apart. The land is rapidly eroded and large amounts of sediment are carried away.

MASSIVE BURIAL

Land animals that had survived the early stages of the advancing catastrophe are progressively buried in the rapidly accumulating layers of sediments on the submerged land masses, which will eventually lead to their fossilization. The entire earth is under water as all life on land is wiped out.

WATERS DOMINATE THE EARTH

Floodwaters cover the entire earth and dominate it for 150 days. The highest hills are covered by water to a depth of at least 15 cubits (greater than 22 feet).

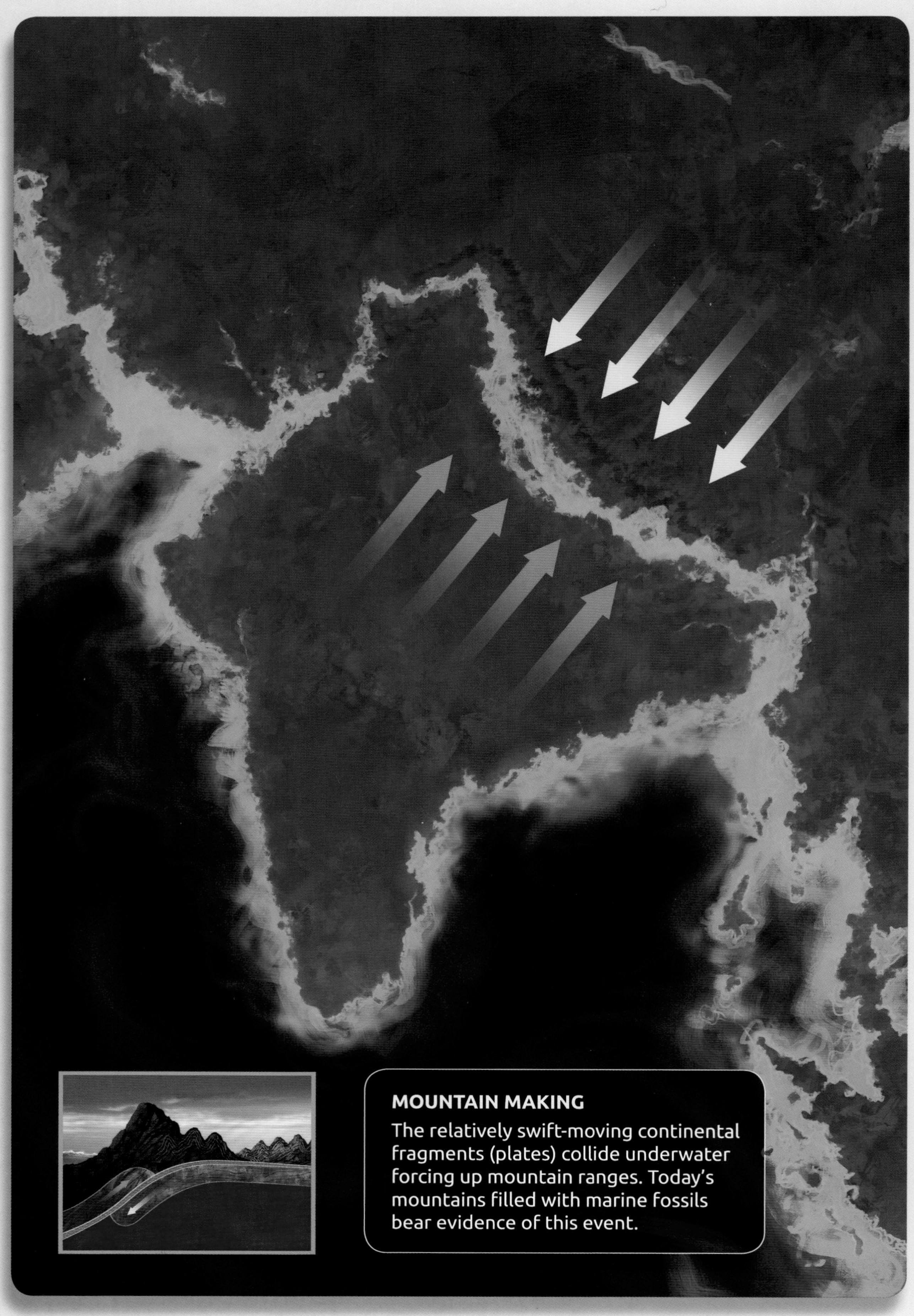

MOUNTAIN MAKING

The relatively swift-moving continental fragments (plates) collide underwater forcing up mountain ranges. Today's mountains filled with marine fossils bear evidence of this event.

THE ARK RESTS

On the 17th day of the seventh month in Noah's 600th year the Ark comes to rest on one of the newly formed mountains in the region of Ararat.

MOUNTAINTOPS VISIBLE

On the first day of the tenth month of Noah's 600th year, the tops of other mountains rise above the water's surface as the waters are also draining away. As land masses continue to rise and waters continue to run off the emerging land surfaces, large amounts of sediment are washed away and canyons are quickly carved into the rock layers.

LEAVING THE ARK

In Noah's 601st year, on the 27th day of the second month, the ground is dry enough for land creatures to live on. Thus approximately one year after boarding, Noah, his family, and all the animals leave the Ark.

INTERPRETING THE EVIDENCE

Creationists and evolutionists study the **same evidence**.
We examine:

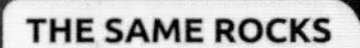

THE SAME FOSSILS

THE SAME WORLD

So why do we reach **different conclusions** about the **same evidence**? Our conclusions are strongly influenced by our **worldviews**.

THE EVOLUTIONARY WORLDVIEW

looks at the rock layers around the world and interprets them as the **result of slow and gradual processes** over the course of **millions and millions of years**.

THE BIBLICAL WORLDVIEW

looks at the same rock layers and sees overwhelming evidence that they were **rapidly** laid down during the **yearlong global Flood described in Genesis.**

Which worldview makes better sense of the evidence?

UNIFORMITARIANISM

Burial During Millions of Years

According to the predominant scientific model, the layers of the geologic column represent hundreds of millions of years of slow and gradual geologic processes. The fossils allegedly show that "simple" organisms progressively developed into more "complex" life forms over long periods of time.

An Interpretation

Holocene
Pleistocene
Pliocene
Miocene
Oligocene
Eocene
Paleocene
Cretaceous
Jurassic
Triassic
Permian
Pennsylvanian
Mississippian
Devonian
Silurian
Ordovician
Cambrian

What We Observe

PROBLEM

Where are all the transitional fossils?

PROBLEM

Why are there time gaps with no erosion between some layers of the column?

PROBLEM

Due to the repeated churning of soil by tiny organisms, a process known as bioturbation, gradual processes of depositing sediments would not permit distinct rock layers to form.

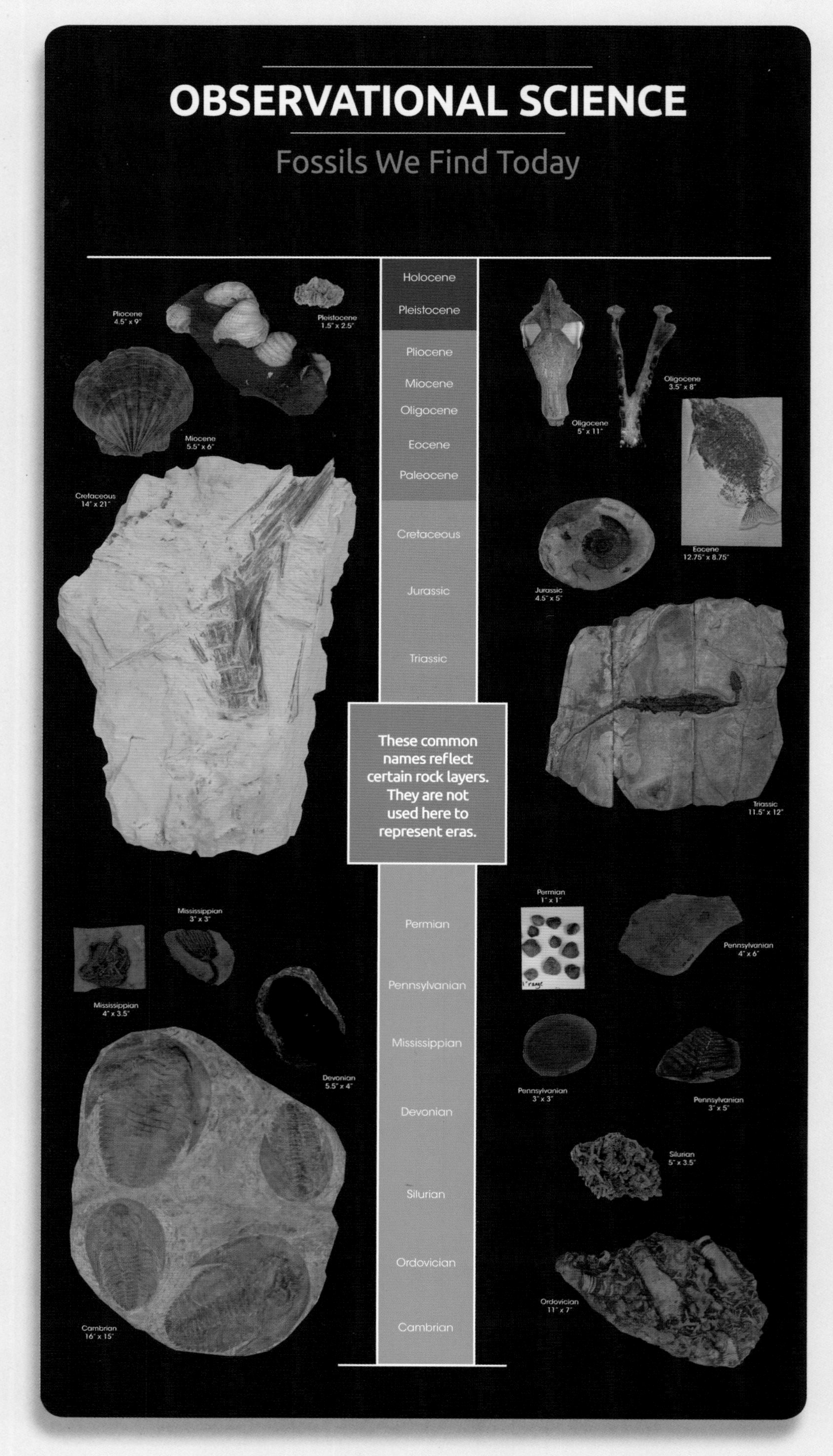
OBSERVATIONAL SCIENCE
Fossils We Find Today
Holocene
Pleistocene
Pliocene
Miocene
Oligocene
Eocene
Paleocene
Cretaceous
Jurassic
Triassic
These common names reflect certain rock layers. They are not used here to represent eras.
Permian
Pennsylvanian
Mississippian
Devonian
Silurian
Ordovician
Cambrian
Pliocene 4.5" x 9"
Pleistocene 1.5" x 2.5"
Miocene 5.5" x 6"
Cretaceous 14" x 21"
Oligocene 5" x 11"
Oligocene 3.5" x 8"
Eocene 12.75" x 8.75"
Jurassic 4.5" x 5"
Triassic 11.5" x 12"
Mississippian 3" x 3"
Mississippian 4" x 3.5"
Devonian 5.5" x 4"
Cambrian 16" x 15"
Permian 1" x 1"
Pennsylvanian 4" x 6"
Pennsylvanian 3" x 3"
Pennsylvanian 3" x 5"
Silurian 5" x 3.5"
Ordovician 11" x 7"

CATASTROPHISM

Burial During the Year of the Flood

The order in which fossils appear in the record can be generally understood as a progression of burial according to the ecosystems in which the creatures lived in the pre-Flood world, although marine fossils are found throughout the record.
Order of Burial as the Waters Rose During the Flood Year
Organisms on the sea floor were buried first, followed by other marine animals and then land-dwelling creatures.

A Creation-Flood model explains that most of the fossil-bearing rock layers were deposited during the Genesis Flood.

WHICH PLANET SUFFERED A MASSIVE CATASTROPHIC FLOOD?

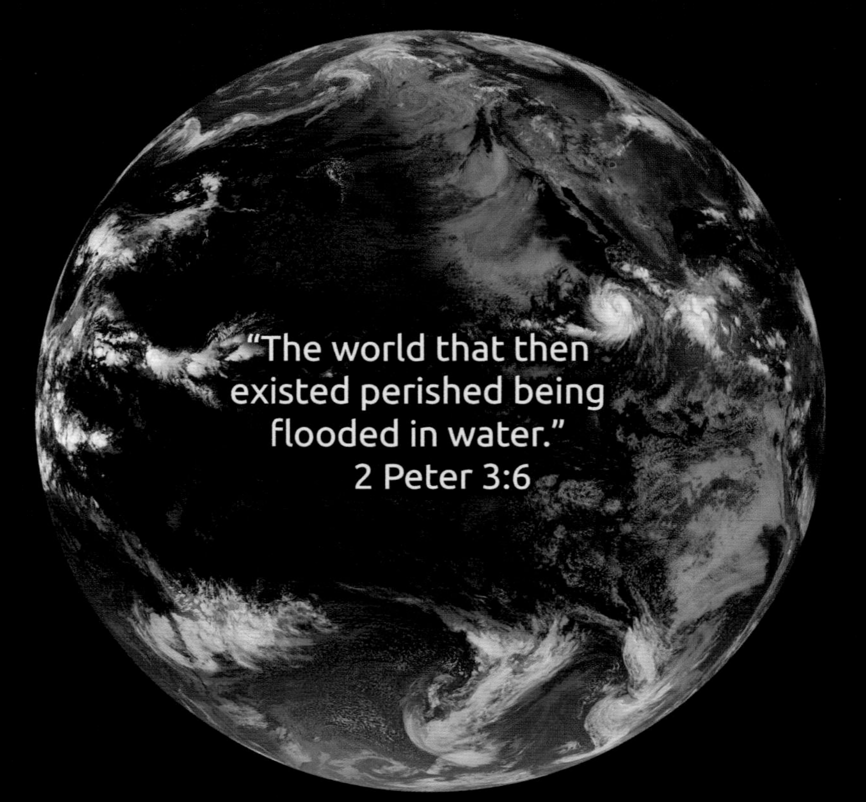

"The world that then existed perished being flooded in water."
2 Peter 3:6

Stranger than Fiction

Despite the fact that there is no known liquid water on the surface of Mars, many scientists believe that Mars once suffered a flood of biblical proportions. Ironically, many of these same scientists deny that Earth, a planet 70% covered with water, ever had a global Flood.

There is powerful evidence to show that both planets suffered major flooding.

EVIDENCES FOR A FLOOD ON MARS

The large Marte Vallis formation (600 miles long, 62 miles wide, 260 feet deep) is believed to be an ancient waterway that has since been covered by lava from volcanic eruptions. Many other features discovered on Mars have led scientists to conclude that the planet underwent flooding in the past.

COMPLEX CHANNELS

Mars Express took this image in 2012 of a steep channel, apparently cut by water. A side channel flows into it.

GRAVEL IN A STREAMBED

In 2012 the *Curiosity* rover found rounded gravel similar to those found in Earth's streambeds. The gravel is too large to be transported and rounded by wind.

DRY RIVERBEDS

The Viking orbiters in the 1970s discovered what appear to be dry riverbeds with branching drainage patterns.

FRESH GULLIES FORMED

In 2000 the *Mars Global Surveyor* discovered what appear to be fresh gullies flowing down the side of a basin. Later information indicated it came from exposed permafrost.

DENYING THE BIBLICAL FLOOD: SCIENCE OR BIAS?

COMPLEX CHANNELS

Canyons all over Earth feature complex channel systems like this one in eastern Egypt.

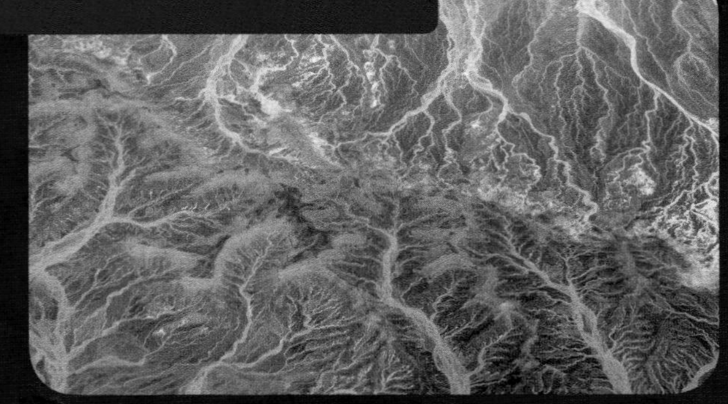

The same type of evidence for massive flooding on Mars can be found in abundance on Earth.

The Earth carries all the hallmarks of a planet that once had a global Flood. The Flood described in Genesis would lay down the vast majority of Earth's fossil-bearing rock layers in a short period of time. Billions of organisms were buried in the process. The remains of these fossilized creatures and the sedimentary layers in which they are found bear witness to this event.

DRY RIVERBEDS

This dry riverbed or wadi from the Negev Desert in Israel is just one of thousands of dry riverbeds found around the world.

Why do so many scientists reject a massive flood on Earth while accepting one on Mars?

The truth is that the worldwide Flood described in Genesis would completely undermine evolutionary beliefs about life on this planet.

The rejection of the biblical Flood is often due to evolutionary biases rather than the actual evidence. In fact, it is not a stretch to think that nearly every geologist would appeal to a global flood to explain many of Earth's features if the Bible had never mentioned such an event.

GRAVEL IN A STREAMBED

The Shinarump Conglomerate Member of the Triassic Chinle Formation in northern Arizona averages 50 feet in thickness and covers an area of at least 100,000 square miles.

RAPID FOSSIL FORMATION

Mother and Baby Buried Together

We are often told that it takes long periods of time to form a fossil. After an animal dies it is slowly buried by sediment. Over thousands or even millions of years, the fossil is formed as minerals in the ground replace the bones and other organic materials of the creature. However, unless they are buried rapidly and preserved, animals decompose after dying. Thus, fossils are known to only form relatively quickly under proper conditions.

An icthyosaur dies during the Flood while giving birth.

The icthyosaurs are rapidly buried by fast-moving sediments during the Flood.

Over time, minerals replace animal tissue, creating a fossil.

Thousands of years later, the fossil is discovered.

CROSS-CONTINENT DEPOSITION

Sediment Layers Deposited Across Continents

Many rock layers stretch across entire continents, and these same layers can be found across other continents as well. For example, the layer of rock called the Tapeats Sandstone in the Grand Canyon can also be found right across North Africa and in Israel. Coal seams, chalk beds, and limestone layers can also extend across several continents. Such widespread layering of materials does not fit with the notion of slow and gradual processes, but it is perfectly consistent with the global Flood described in Genesis.

How do we know the Tapeats Sandstone can be correlated with the Mt. Simon Sandstone, the Sauk Sandstone, and the Amudei Shelomo Sandstone?

- In addition to their location at the bottom of the pile of sedimentary layers and sitting on top of eroded-off crystalline basement rocks, these sandstone layers share four features that help us understand that they were deposited at the same time on a global scale.
- **Grain Sizes**: These layers are made up of the same suite of sand-sized grains.
- **Fossil Content**: These layers contain the same types of fossils, such as trilobites.
- **Minerals and Chemistry**: Each layer of sandstone has a distinct chemical makeup. Like other sandstones, these layers consist mostly of quartz, but unlike other sandstones, they also contain the mineral feldspar.
- **Sedimentary Features**: Sedimentary layers often display features such as cross-beds that reveal the direction and speed of the water flow that deposited the sand. These "fossil waves" indicate that the Tapeats, Mt. Simon, Sauk, and Amudei Shelomo sandstones were formed in the same way.

POLYSTRATE FOSSILS

Upright Trees Buried by Many Layers

Polystrate fossils are found around the world. For example, certain fossilized trees, some of which are upside down, extend through many feet of rock layers. Slow and gradual processes cannot account for the build-up of sediment layers around the upright trees before they rotted. A more reasonable explanation is that the trees were buried rapidly as a result of catastrophic sediment deposition.

CATASTROPHIC DEVASTATION

Thousands of logs cover Spirit Lake following the eruption of Mt. St. Helens.

NATURAL PROCESSES

Logs eventually become waterlogged and float mostly upright.

UPRIGHT BURIAL

Logs sink to the lakebed at different times and are buried progressively in a standing position.

EVIDENCE OF CATASTROPHE

Specimen Ridge at Yellowstone shows scores of upright logs buried in the same manner as at Spirit Lake.

PARACONFORMITIES

Millions of Years Without Erosion?

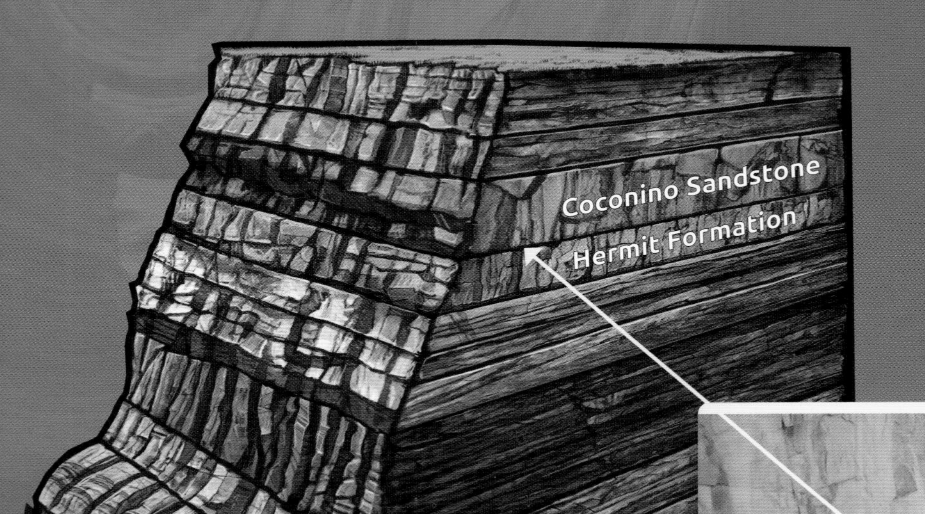

one WORLD two VIEWS

WHAT WE OBSERVE

After the Hermit Formation in the Grand Canyon was laid down, at least five million years are supposed to have passed before the Coconino Sandstone was deposited above it. Yet there is no evidence of erosion between the two layers. A better conclusion is that these rocks were laid down in rapid succession during the Flood.

MILLIONS OF YEARS

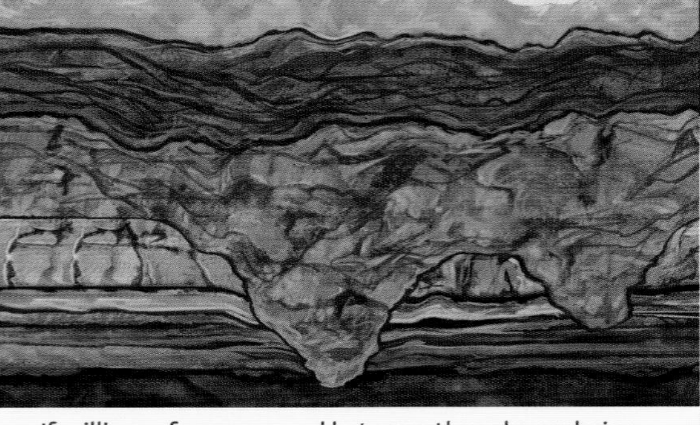

If millions of years passed between these layers being laid down, then erosional features would be present.

YEAR OF THE FLOOD

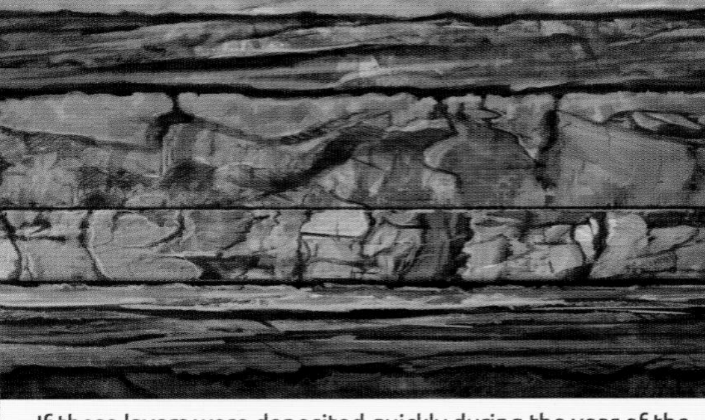

If these layers were deposited quickly during the year of the Flood, then rapid or no erosional features would be seen.

WARPED ROCKS

Rock Layer Sequences Deposited Rapidly Before Being Bent

Evidence for rapidly deposited rock layers can be seen in locations where whole rock layer sequences have been bent without fracturing. When we find multiple layers of rock that are warped without fracturing or breaking it indicates that all of these layers were deposited over a short period of time (rather than the supposed hundreds of millions of years) and were bent before hardening.

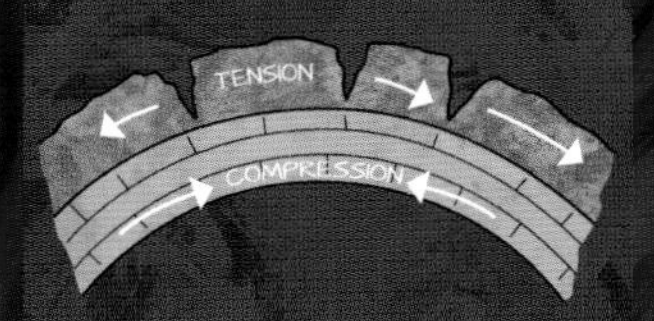

Hardened rock layers break when bent.

It is claimed there is 130–140 million years of alleged time missing at this boundary, but both layers are bent smoothly without breaking.

It is claimed this rock layer was bent 450 million years after it was deposited, but it is bent smoothly.

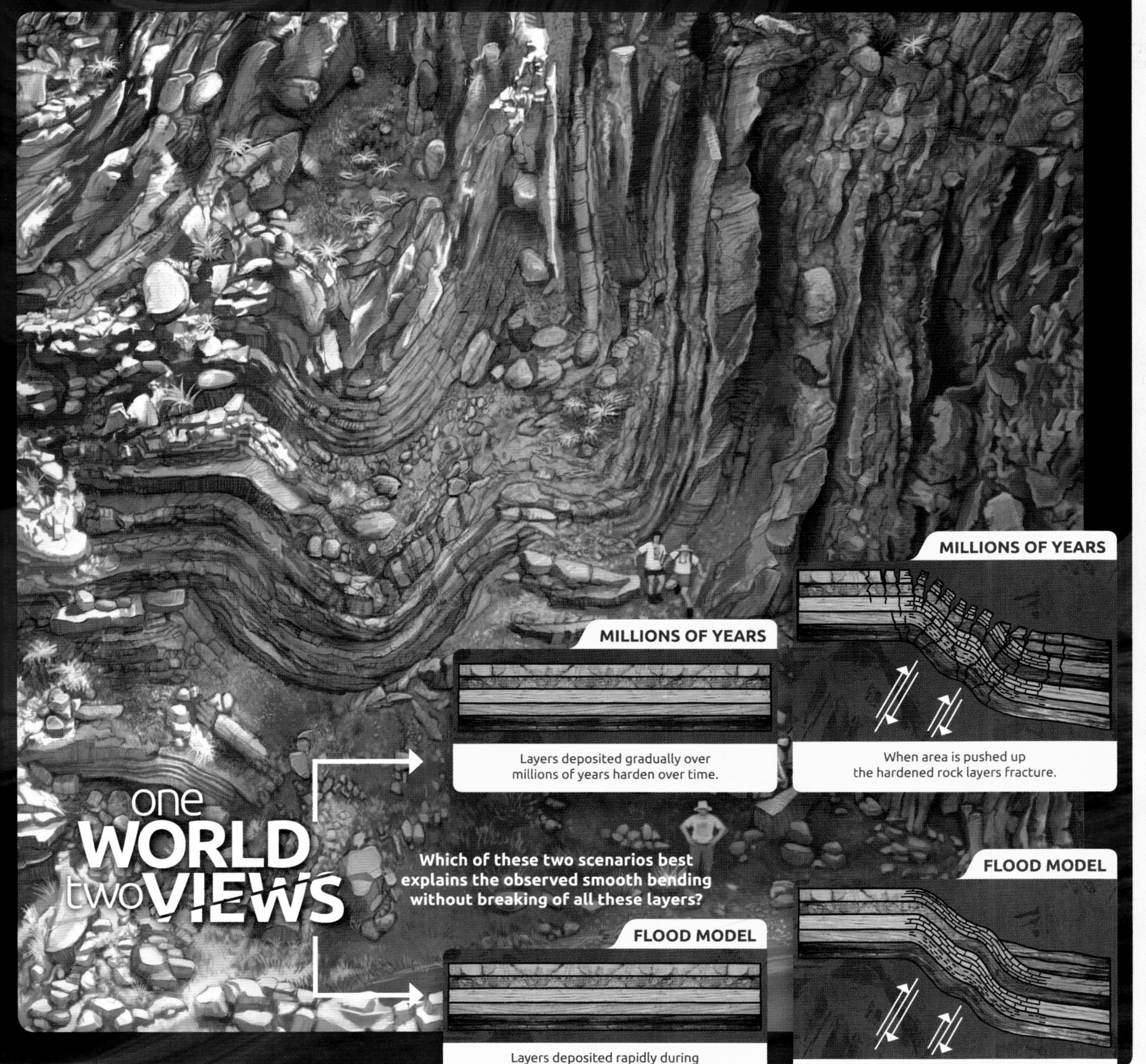

MILLIONS OF YEARS
Layers deposited gradually over millions of years harden over time.
MILLIONS OF YEARS
When area is pushed up the hardened rock layers fracture.
one WORLD two VIEWS
Which of these two scenarios best explains the observed smooth bending without breaking of all these layers?
FLOOD MODEL
Layers deposited rapidly during the Flood and remain soft for a time.
FLOOD MODEL
When area is pushed up the soft layers bend and warp without fracturing.

THE GRAND CANYON

How Was This Famous Canyon Formed?

VERTICAL WALLS

The high vertical walls of many canyons show that they were carved quickly. If they were cut slowly over long periods of time, the walls would be sloped due to years of erosional forces.

LACK OF TALUS DEPOSITS

Many canyons have a small amount of debris, called talus, at the base of their cliffs. Over millions of years, large amounts of talus would have accumulated. The lack of talus signifies that the debris was carried away as the canyon was rapidly carved by a larger volume of water than what currently flows through it.

SCALE OF RIVER TO CANYON

Most canyons are many times wider than the river that flows through their base. This indicates that the amount of water responsible for cutting through the rocks was much greater than the current flow.

16 MILES WIDE

Representation of the Grand Canyon

ENGINEERS CANYON

Steve Austin

Approximately 1/40 the size of the Grand Canyon, this 100-foot deep gorge was not slowly carved by the North Fork of the Toutle River. The "Little Grand Canyon" was cut out by hot water and volcanic ash mixed as a mud flow on March 19, 1982.

Popular models of canyon formation explain that they are cut by relatively small amounts of water over long periods of time through slow and gradual processes. However, we have observed many canyons being formed by large amounts of water in days rather than eons.

FOSSILS AND THE BIBLE

THE BIBLICAL POSITION

God creates man and calls Creation very good

Man's sin corrupts Creation, bringing death, suffering, and disease

Floodwaters cover all the highest mountains under the whole heaven

Billions of creatures killed and buried by the Flood

In a misguided attempt to blend biblical teaching with the popular idea that earth is millions of years old, some Christians have invented imaginative ways to reinterpret the Bible's creation account. However, every concept they have developed, such as the gap theory, progressive creationism, the framework hypothesis, and the day-age theory, is littered with problems.

THE OLD-EARTH POSITION

Death, suffering, and disease for millions of years

God creates and calls death, suffering, and disease very good

Man's sin has virtually no effect on Creation

This is what a mountain-covering local flood would look like

PROBLEM

Old-earth views necessarily force millions of years of thorns, death, suffering, and disease before Adam and Eve. Yet, after God created the first two people, the Bible states everything He had made was "very good" (Genesis 1:31).

PROBLEM

To be consistent, the old-earth positions must reinterpret the Genesis Flood as a regional or tranquil event. Yet the Bible clearly describes the mountain-covering Flood as global in extent and its waters as very powerful.

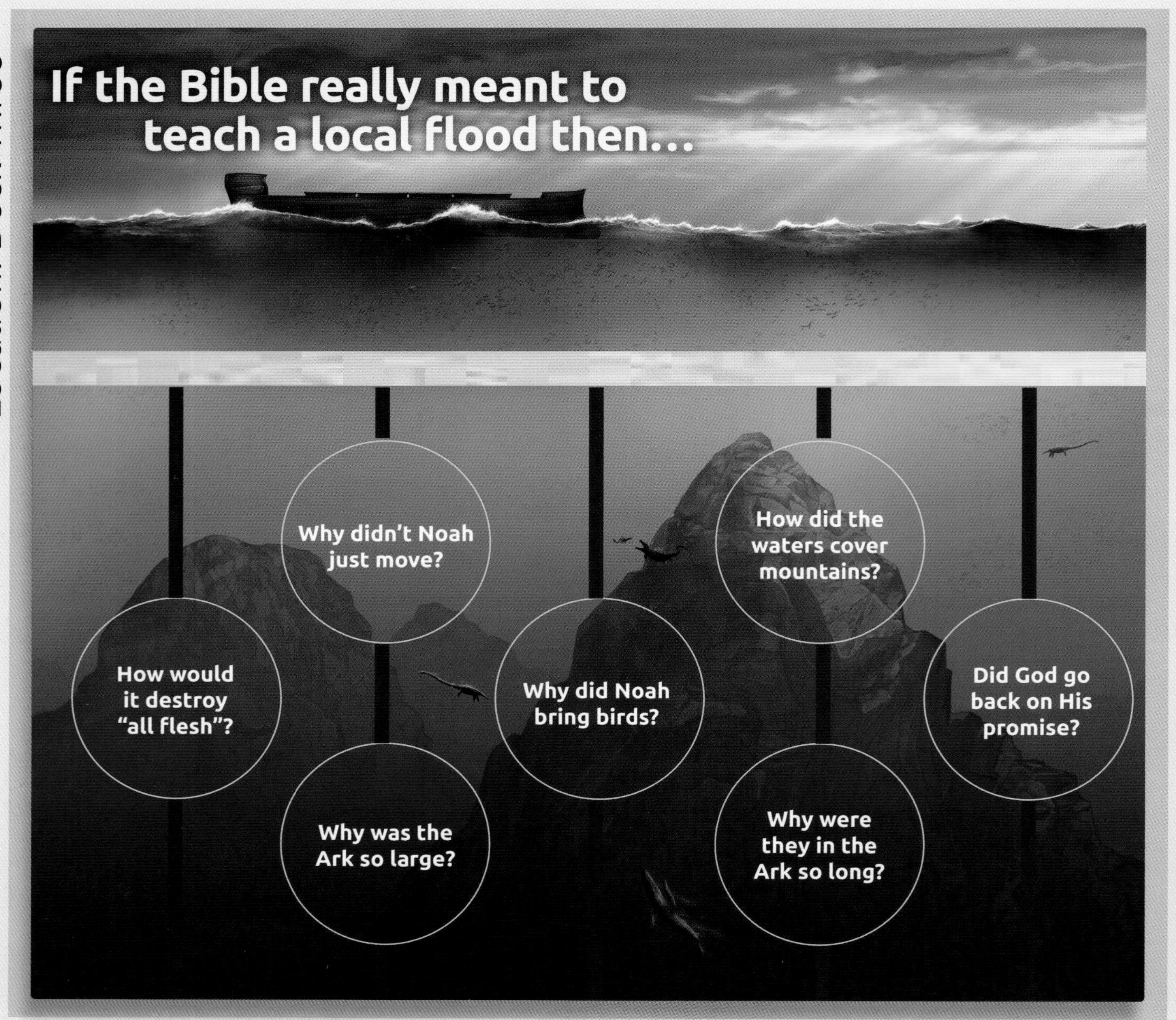

If the Bible really meant to teach a local flood then...
Why didn't Noah just move?
How did the waters cover mountains?
How would it destroy "all flesh"?
Why did Noah bring birds?
Did God go back on His promise?
Why was the Ark so large?
Why were they in the Ark so long?

If the Bible really meant to teach a local flood then...

Why would Noah need to build an Ark if the Flood were just a regional event? The animals and people could have easily moved out of the area before the Flood began.

The Bible states that the waters of the Flood covered the highest point to a depth of 15 cubits. Once the waters cover the highest mountain, it can no longer be a local flood.

God stated that the purpose of the Flood was to destroy "all flesh" that lived on the land. This phrase is used thirteen times in the Flood account, stressing the worldwide extent of the devastation.

Why would Noah bring flying creatures aboard the Ark if the Flood were a regional event? They could have easily flown out of the area.

God said the rainbow would be a sign that He would never send another Flood like the one in Genesis. Yet, if it were merely a regional flood, then God has broken that promise repeatedly.

The Ark was large enough to house pairs of every kind of land animal on the planet. If the Flood were only a local or regional event, then the Ark could have been much smaller.

Noah's family was aboard the Ark for about a year. This is far too long for any local flood and only makes sense with a global Flood.

THE ICE AGE
AN AFTEREFFECT OF THE GLOBAL FLOOD
The global Flood devastated the entire earth and left evidence in the form of fossils and sedimentary layers around the world. Repercussions of this catastrophe rocked the planet for many decades as the unique conditions of the Flood plunged the earth into the Ice Age. Rapidly changing environments brought difficult challenges for living creatures as they endeavored to fill new surroundings.

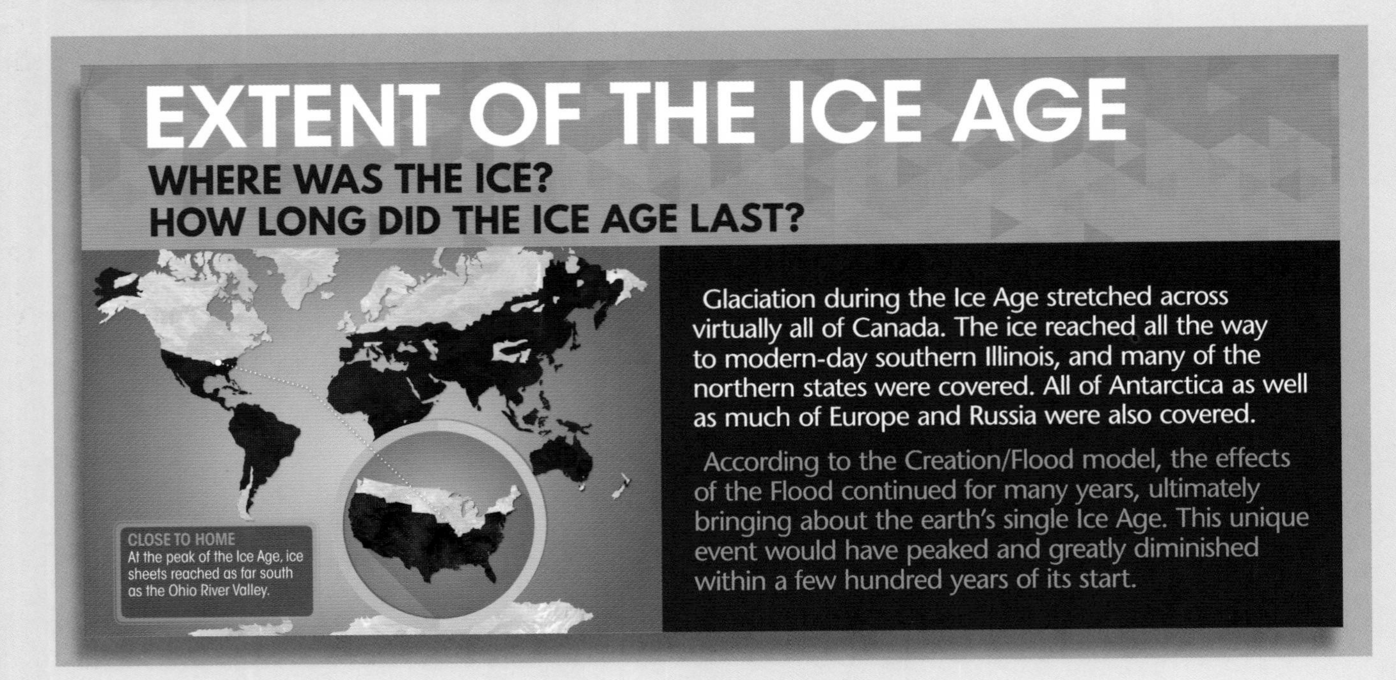
EXTENT OF THE ICE AGE
WHERE WAS THE ICE?
HOW LONG DID THE ICE AGE LAST?
CLOSE TO HOME
At the peak of the Ice Age, ice sheets reached as far south as the Ohio River Valley.
Glaciation during the Ice Age stretched across virtually all of Canada. The ice reached all the way to modern-day southern Illinois, and many of the northern states were covered. All of Antarctica as well as much of Europe and Russia were also covered.
According to the Creation/Flood model, the effects of the Flood continued for many years, ultimately bringing about the earth's single Ice Age. This unique event would have peaked and greatly diminished within a few hundred years of its start.

ONE ICE AGE OR MANY?

DIFFERENT WORLDVIEWS LEAD TO DIFFERENT CONCLUSIONS

BIBLICAL VIEW

Our *biblical model* maintains that there was only one ice age, and it came about as a result of the global Flood.

SECULAR VIEW

The leading *secular model* holds that there were at least four major ice ages, each exhibiting periods of glaciers advancing and retreating.

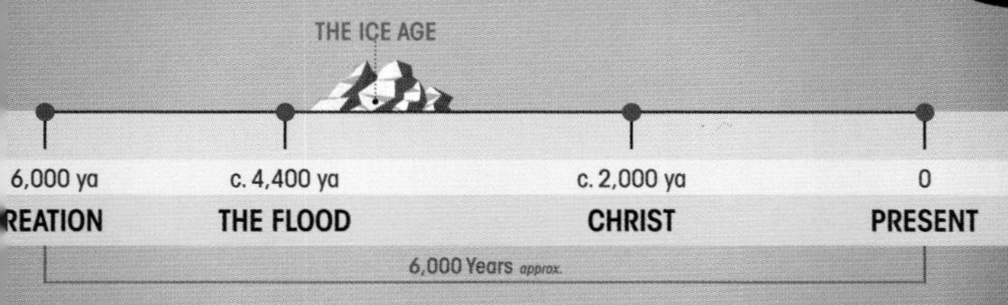

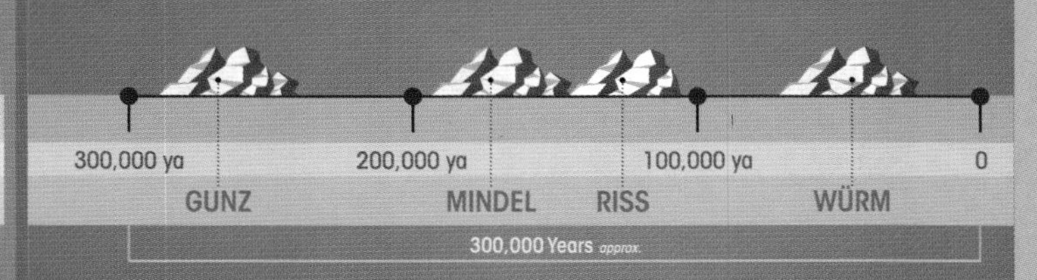

LAND BRIDGES

HOW COULD LAND ANIMALS REACH DISTANT PLACES?

After the Flood, massive volumes of water would have remained on the land masses in inland seas, long since drained or dried up. Tremendous amounts of water were trapped in the buildup of snow and ice on land. With so much water removed from the ocean, sea levels would have been hundreds of feet lower, exposing land bridges to nearly every continent on the globe.

In addition to these natural bridges, land animals could have reached distant shores via other means, including swimming, floating debris, and with people on boats.

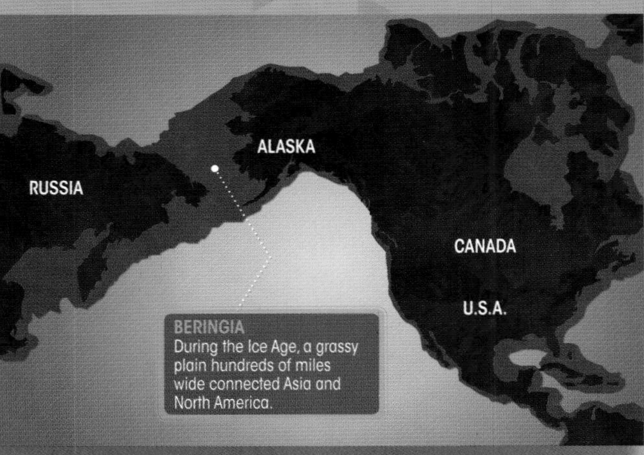

ALASKA
RUSSIA
CANADA
U.S.A.
BERINGIA
During the Ice Age, a grassy plain hundreds of miles wide connected Asia and North America.

ICE AGE MECHANISM

HOW WOULD THE GLOBAL FLOOD TRIGGER THE ICE AGE?

WARMER OCEANS

At the start of the Flood, massive fissures formed in the sea floor, allowing magma to contact ocean water. This created enormous steam jets that raced to the surface, spraying ocean water hundreds of feet into the atmosphere. These processes greatly increased the ocean temperature, and combined with volcanic activity on land, filled the sky with pollutants.

COOLER ATMOSPHERE

As a result of volcanic and geyser activity, the upper atmosphere filled with pollutants, preventing a large amount of sunlight from reaching the earth's surface. This activity drastically reduced air temperatures over the interiors of the continents around the planet while ocean temperatures remained much higher.

GREATER SNOWFALL

Significantly warmer ocean temperatures produced considerably higher amounts of evaporation. Due to the cooler air temperatures in the continental interiors, great amounts of precipitation fell as snow on such land areas in the higher latitudes. Over several decades, massive ice sheets and glaciers grew. After perhaps two centuries as the volcanic activity subsided, the air pollutants were removed, and air and water temperatures returned over several more decades to today's "normal."

GIANTS OF THE ICE AGE

WHY DID ICE AGE ANIMALS GROW SO LARGE?

The fossil record reveals that many Ice Age animals grew larger than their ancestors from the time of the Flood. Why would these creatures increase in size in colder climates?

During cooler conditions, larger animals generally have many survival advantages over the smaller representatives within the same kind.

- Larger animals are usually better at intimidating predators.
- Larger animals often move faster.
- Larger animals typically stay warmer due to an advantageous surface area-to-volume ratio.
- Larger animals tend to live longer.
- Larger animals require less food per pound.

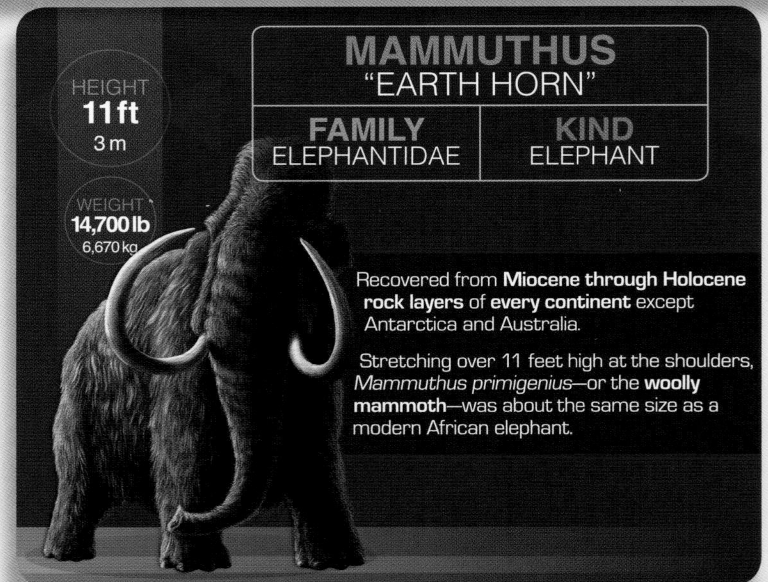

MAMMUTHUS
"EARTH HORN"
FAMILY
ELEPHANTIDAE
KIND
ELEPHANT
HEIGHT
11 ft
3 m
WEIGHT
14,700 lb
6,670 kg
Recovered from Miocene through Holocene rock layers of every continent except Antarctica and Australia.
Stretching over 11 feet high at the shoulders, Mammuthus primigenius—or the woolly mammoth—was about the same size as a modern African elephant.

GIGANTOPITHECUS
"GIANT APE"
FAMILY
PONGIDAE
KIND
GREAT APE
HEIGHT
10 ft
3 m
WEIGHT
1,200 lb
540 kg
Recovered from Pleistocene rock layers of Southeast Asia.
Standing up to 10 feet tall and weighing more than two gorillas, Gigantopithecus blacki was the largest known ape.

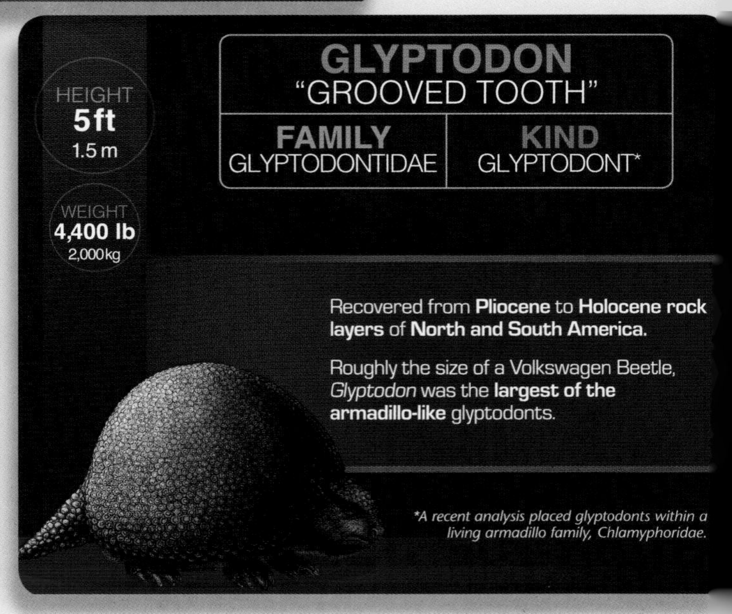

GLYPTODON
"GROOVED TOOTH"
FAMILY
GLYPTODONTIDAE
KIND
GLYPTODONT*
HEIGHT
5 ft
1.5 m
WEIGHT
4,400 lb
2,000 kg
Recovered from Pliocene to Holocene rock layers of North and South America.
Roughly the size of a Volkswagen Beetle, Glyptodon was the largest of the armadillo-like glyptodonts.
*A recent analysis placed glyptodonts within a living armadillo family, Chlamyphoridae.

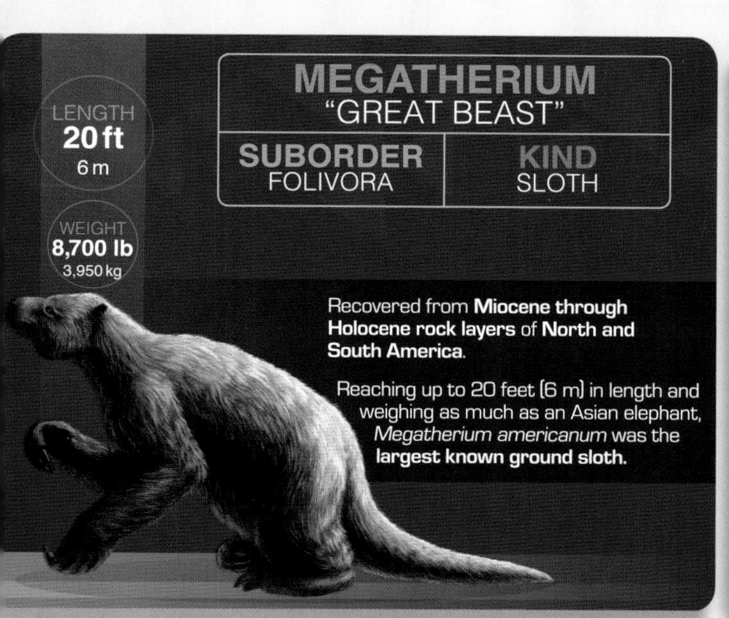

LENGTH
20 ft
6 m
WEIGHT
8,700 lb
3,950 kg
MEGATHERIUM
"GREAT BEAST"
SUBORDER
FOLIVORA
KIND
SLOTH
Recovered from **Miocene through Holocene rock layers** of **North and South America**.
Reaching up to 20 feet (6 m) in length and weighing as much as an Asian elephant, *Megatherium americanum* was the **largest known ground sloth.**

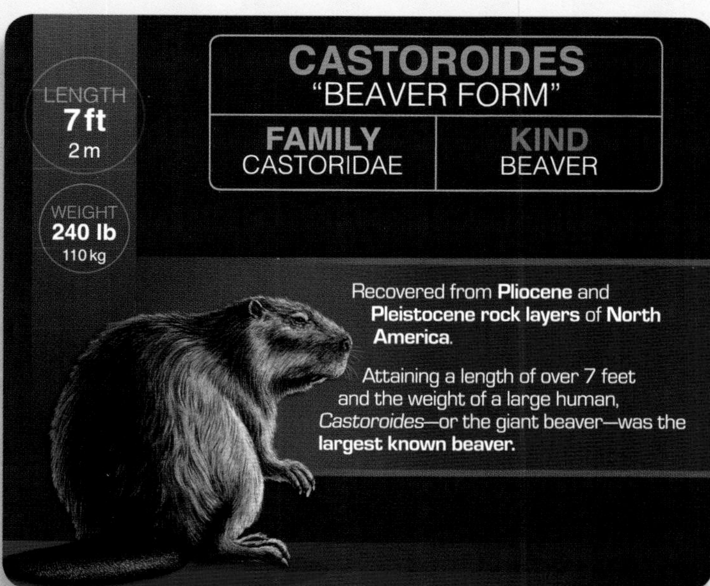

LENGTH
7 ft
2 m
WEIGHT
240 lb
110 kg
CASTOROIDES
"BEAVER FORM"
FAMILY
CASTORIDAE
KIND
BEAVER
Recovered from **Pliocene** and **Pleistocene rock layers** of **North America**.
Attaining a length of over 7 feet and the weight of a large human, *Castoroides*—or the giant beaver—was the **largest known beaver.**

GLACIAL EFFECTS

HOW A GLACIER RESHAPES THE LAND

Glaciers are responsible for many landforms we observe today. As the massive ice sheet advances and retreats, it tends to flatten most of the earth beneath it but leaves behind some telltale signs of its presence.

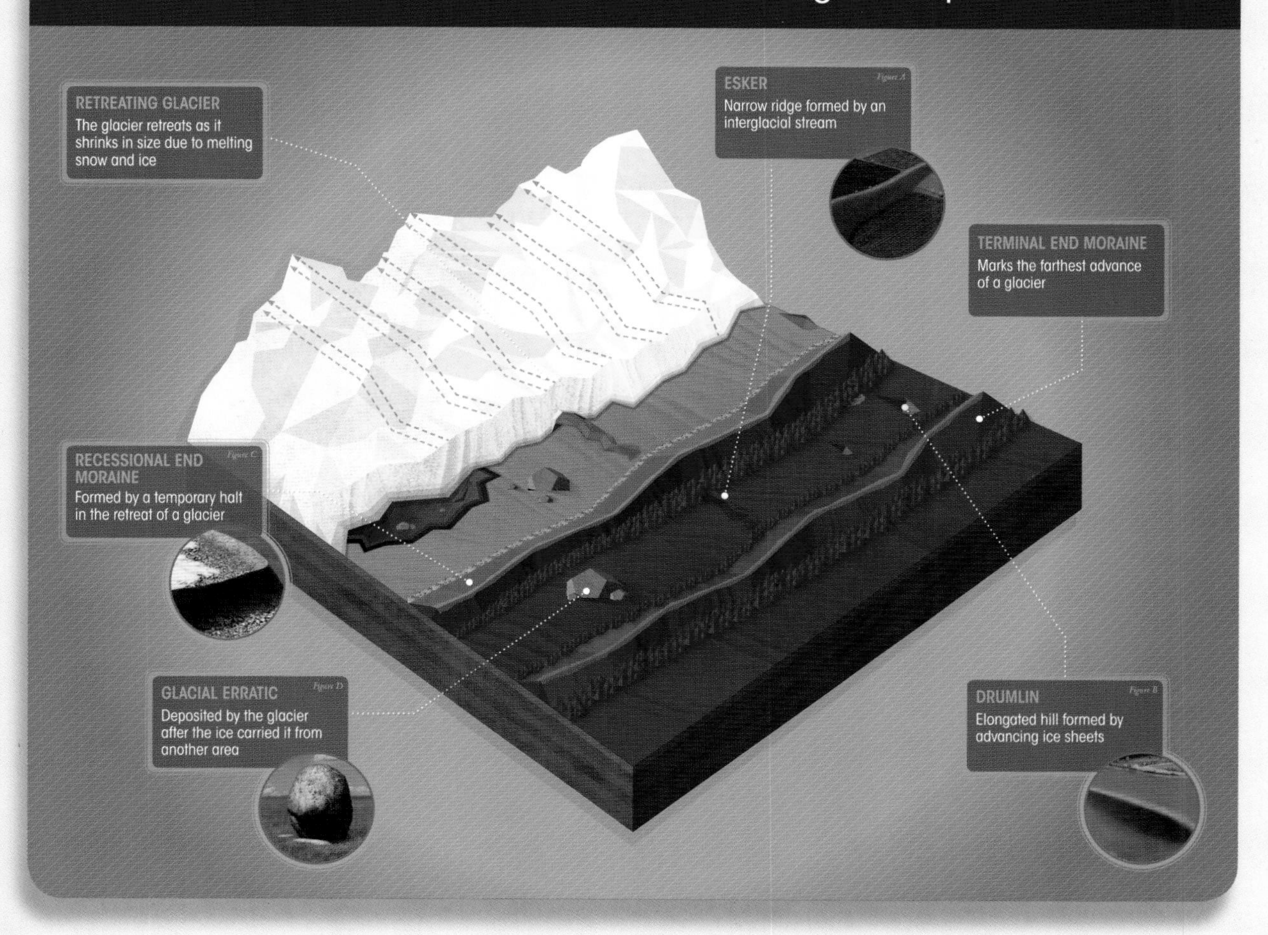

RETREATING GLACIER
The glacier retreats as it shrinks in size due to melting snow and ice

TERMINAL END MORAINE
Marks the farthest advance of a glacier
RECESSIONAL END MORAINE
Formed by a temporary halt in the retreat of a glacier

Deposited by the glacier after the ice carried it from another area

WAS THERE REALLY AN ICE AGE?

REMNANTS OF THE ICE AGE FOUND THROUGHOUT THE HIGHER LATITUDES OF THE NORTHERN AND SOUTHERN HEMISPHERES

ESKER

A narrow ridge of gravel, boulders, and earth deposited under a glacier by an interglacial stream.

DRUMLIN

An elongated hill composed primarily of clay, sand, gravel, and boulders. Drumlins are thought to have been formed by advancing ice sheets.

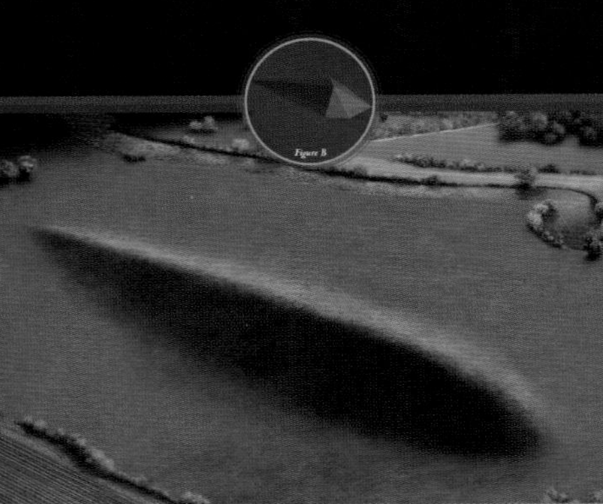

MORAINE

An accumulation of rocks and soil that were carried and deposited by a glacie Terminal moraines are formed at the point of a glacier's maximum advance.

GLACIAL ERRATIC

A rock or boulder differing in mineral makeup from the surrounding rocks. Erratics were transported by glacier-ice to their current resting spot, often having been carried dozens of miles from their source.

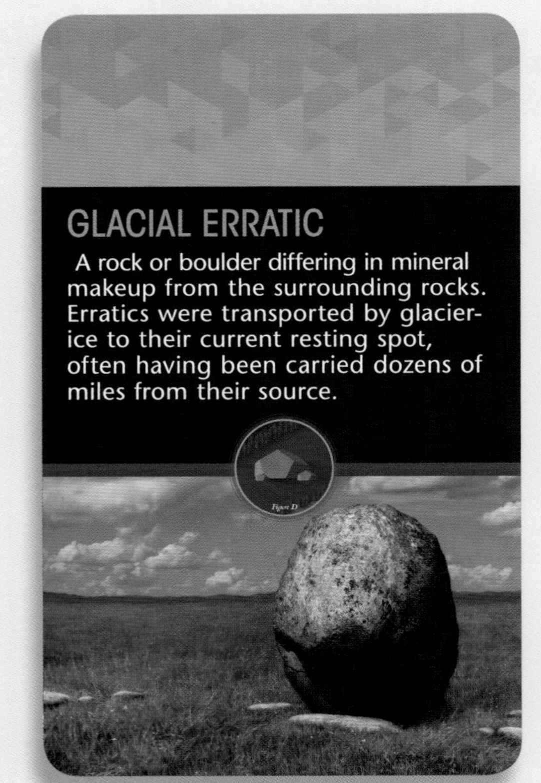

THE LOST SQUADRON

DEEP FREEZE CONSISTENT WITH CREATION/FLOOD ICE AGE MODEL

In 1942, six P-38 fighter planes and two B-17 bombers were forced to land on the ice of Greenland. The planes were abandoned and practically forgotten. Nearly 40 years later a search was made to recover the planes, but they were not located until 1988 when advanced radar spotted them 250 feet beneath the surface.

This diorama depicts the recovery of one of the P-38 fighters. In 1992 an expedition bored a hole into the ice and retrieved the plane piece by piece. Now known as Glacier Girl, this plane has been restored and was flown once again in 2002.

The fact that these aircraft were buried under more than 250 feet of snow and ice in less than 50 years reveals the unreliability of using so-called annual layers as a dating method. The bore hole from the Lost Squadron expedition revealed far more than 50 "annual" layers because multiple layers can form every year. Observational science supports the biblical timeline and contradicts popular teaching about millions of years.

Six P-38s and two B-17s were forced to land on Greenland's ice due to poor weather.

The first plane to land flipped due to the uneven surface, so other planes touched down without using landing gear.

In 1988, the planes were located under 250 feet of ice.

IS CLIMATE CHANGE NATURAL?

WHAT IMPACT DOES MAN HAVE ON GLOBAL TEMPERATURES?

No one denies that climates have changed. But is man responsible for causing rising temperatures? Is the average worldwide temperature even rising? Numerous factors contribute to global weather patterns—sunspot activity, greenhouse gases, volcanism—and experts can be found on either side of the climate debate.

Manmade greenhouse gas emissions were certainly not responsible for two major periods of climate change centuries ago. The Medieval Warm Period (c. AD 800–1200) saw warmer than average temperatures that were even higher than the warmest years of the past few decades. The Little Ice Age (c. AD 1400–1880) brought cooler average temperatures than those experienced in modern times.

This chart shows average temperatures for the past 2,000 years, featuring the Medieval Warm Period and the Little Ice Age. Before the mid-1800s, there was little change in the amount of atmospheric carbon dioxide. So what caused these fluctuations?

*Represents global temperature reconstruction with 95% confidence intervals**

**Loehle and McCulloch (2008)*

***Figures for years 1936–2000 from NOAA's National Climatic Data Center*

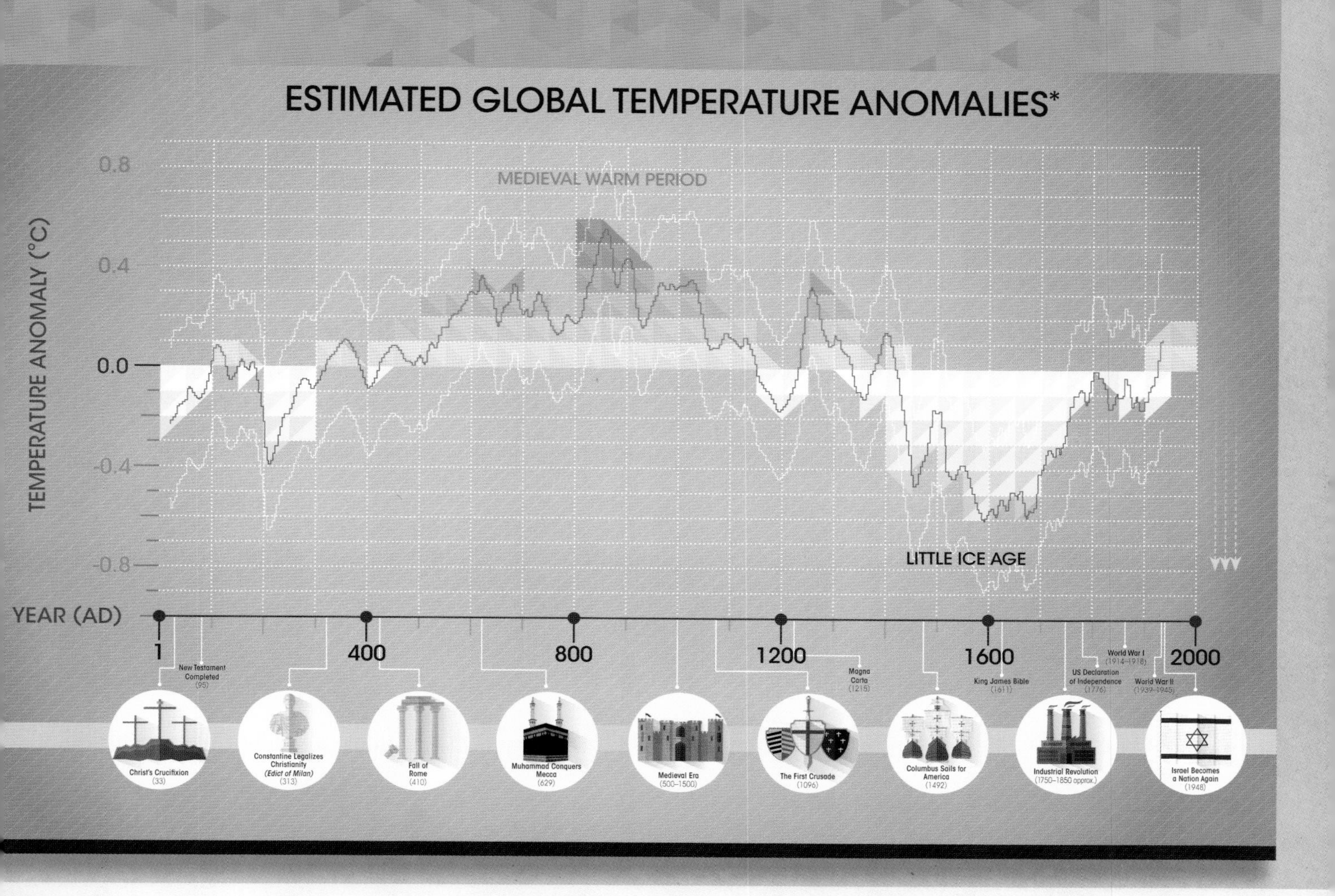
ESTIMATED GLOBAL TEMPERATURE ANOMALIES*
TEMPERATURE ANOMALY (°C)
0.8
0.4
0.0
-0.4
-0.8
MEDIEVAL WARM PERIOD
LITTLE ICE AGE
YEAR (AD)
1
400
800
1200
1600
2000
New Testament Completed (95)
Christ's Crucifixion (33)
Constantine Legalizes Christianity (Edict of Milan) (313)
Fall of Rome (410)
Muhammad Conquers Mecca (629)
Medieval Era (500–1500)
The First Crusade (1096)
Magna Carta (1215)
Columbus Sails for America (1492)
King James Bible (1611)
Industrial Revolution (1750–1850 approx.)
US Declaration of Independence (1776)
World War I (1914–1918)
World War II (1939–1945)
Israel Becomes a Nation Again (1948)

Be FRUITFUL *and* MULTIPLY

God's COMMAND

After the Flood, Noah's descendants spoke one language. The Lord told them to multiply and fill the earth. They fulfilled the first part of this command as the world's population quickly grew. Unlike the animals that spread out to every corner of the globe, the people stayed together, refusing to fill the earth.

Let us BUILD *a* CITY *and a* TOWER

Man's REBELLION

In direct rebellion to God's command to fill the earth, the people gathered together in the plain of Shinar. They desired to make a name for themselves and decided to build a city with a tower whose top reached into the heavens.

So THE LORD SCATTERED *the* PEOPLE

God's JUDGMENT

Since the people refused to scatter, God put an end to their rebellion and accomplished His purpose by confusing their language. No longer able to communicate with each other, the people abandoned their efforts and departed from Babel. The Table of Nations in ***Genesis 10*** names the people groups that filled the earth.

"Come, let us go down and confuse their language so they will be unable to understand one another. So the LORD scattered them across the face of the earth."

— Genesis 11:7–8 —

The ORIGIN *of* LANGUAGES:

Researchers estimate that our languages derived from about 90 language families, a total that will likely decrease with further study.

Biblical MODEL *LANGUAGE ORCHARD*

This data is entirely consistent with the Bible. ***Genesis 10–11*** describes God's confusing of man's language at Babel, and the estimated number of language families is close to the same number of people groups that departed from Babel.

- ***God creates root languages at Babel***
- ***Modern languages develop over time from original language families created at Babel***

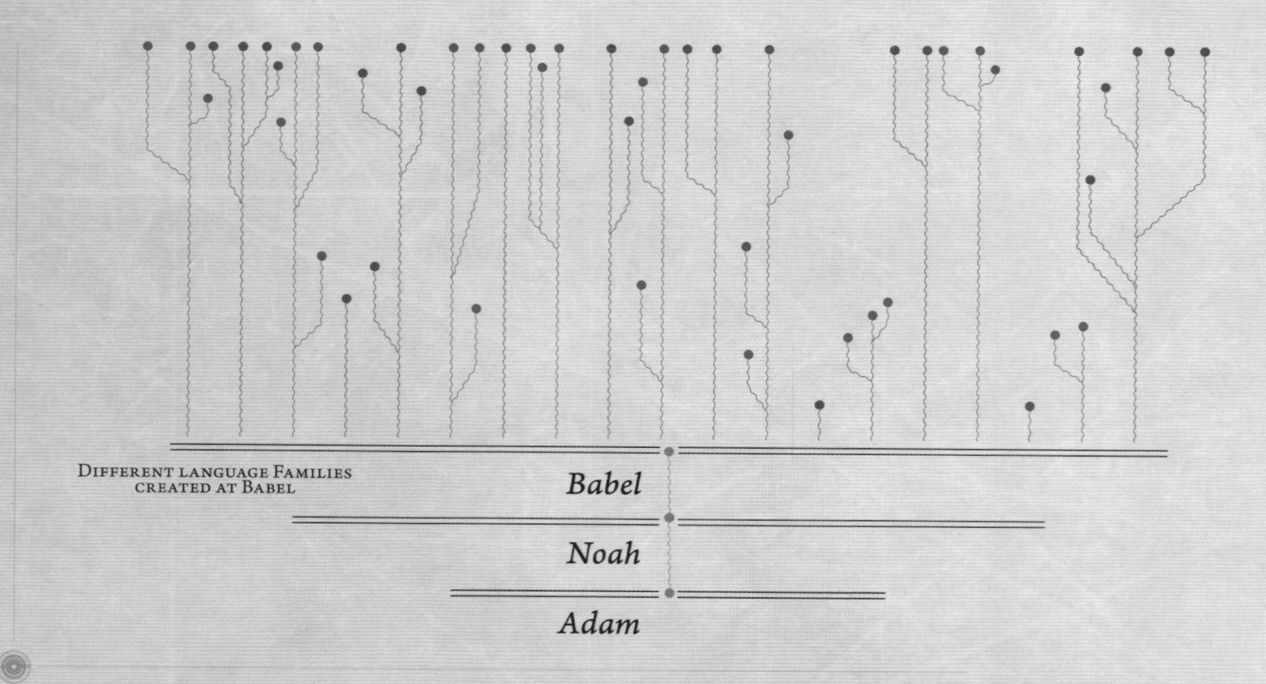

Same EVIDENCE, *Two* VIEWS

Evolutionary MODEL *LANGUAGE TREE*

While evolutionists have developed explanations for the origin of language and language families, these explanations are inconsistent with the idea that humans all share a common ancestor. It seems that the language families would all be traced back to a few groups instead of 90.

- ***Original human language evolves from non-language***
- ***Language families evolve from original language and eventually develop into modern languages***

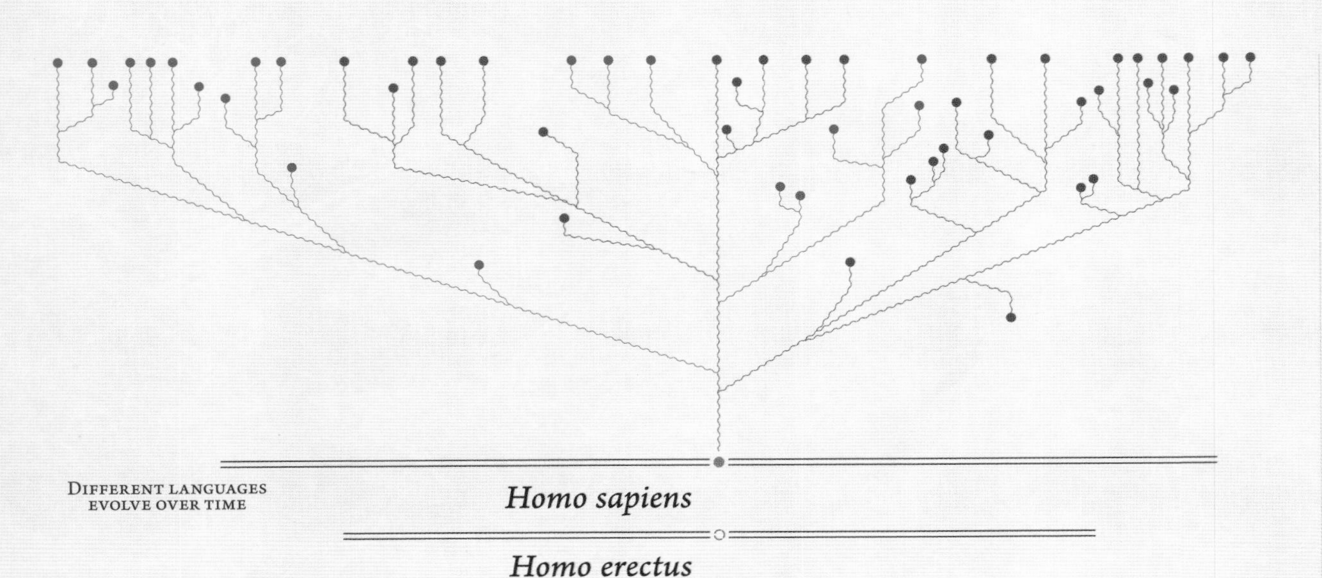

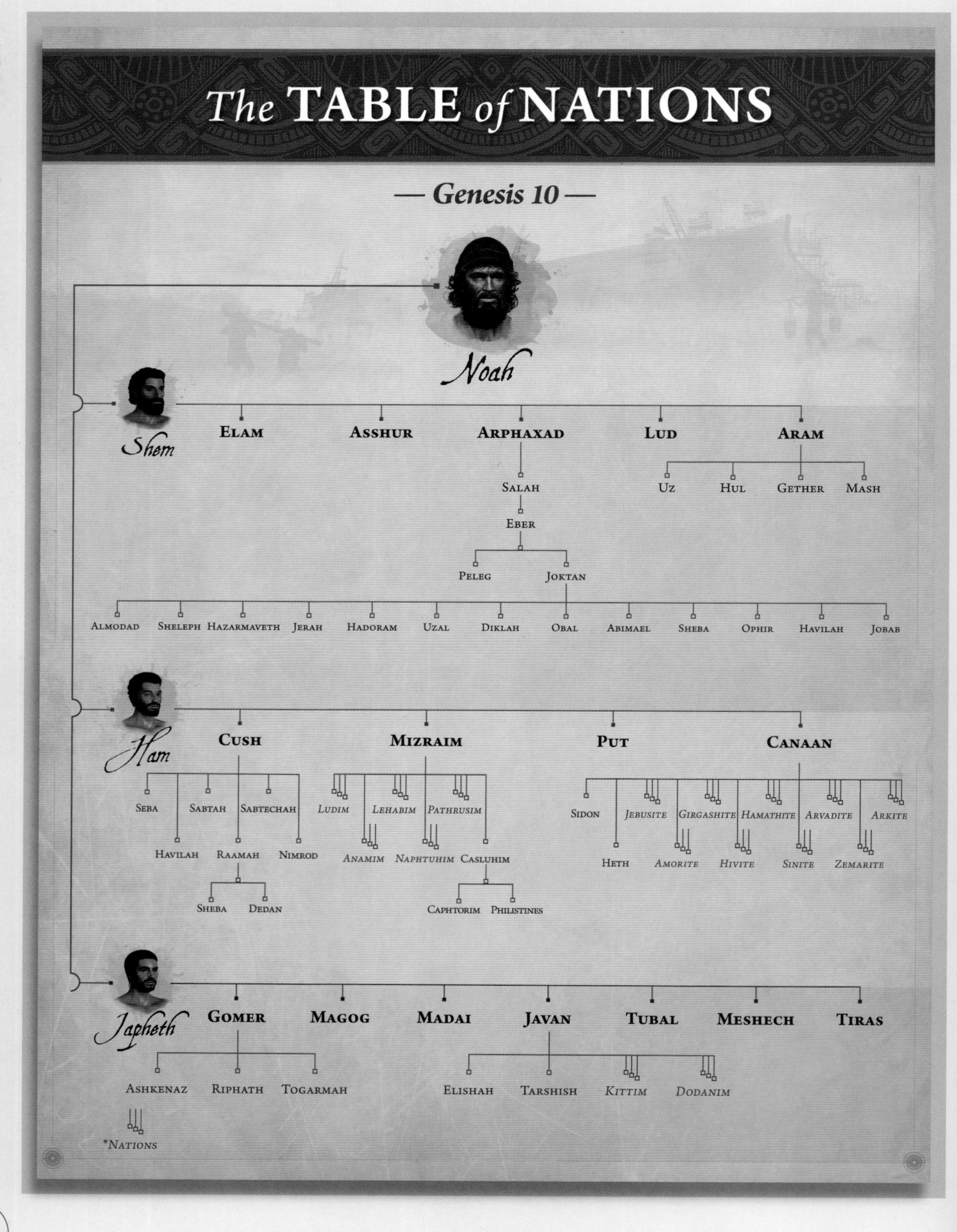
The TABLE of NATIONS
— Genesis 10 —
Noah
Shem
Elam
Asshur
Arphaxad
Lud
Aram
Salah
Uz
Hul
Gether
Mash
Eber
Peleg
Joktan
Almodad
Sheleph
Hazarmaveth
Jerah
Hadoram
Uzal
Diklah
Obal
Abimael
Sheba
Ophir
Havilah
Jobab
Ham
Cush
Mizraim
Put
Canaan
Seba
Sabtah
Sabtechah
Havilah
Raamah
Nimrod
Sheba
Dedan
Ludim
Lehabim
Pathrusim
Anamim
Naphtuhim
Casluhim
Caphtorim
Philistines
Sidon
Jebusite
Girgashite
Hamathite
Arvadite
Arkite
Heth
Amorite
Hivite
Sinite
Zemarite
Japheth
Gomer
Magog
Madai
Javan
Tubal
Meshech
Tiras
Ashkenaz
Riphath
Togarmah
Elishah
Tarshish
Kittim
Dodanim
*Nations

Was the BIBLE Used to Promote RACISM?

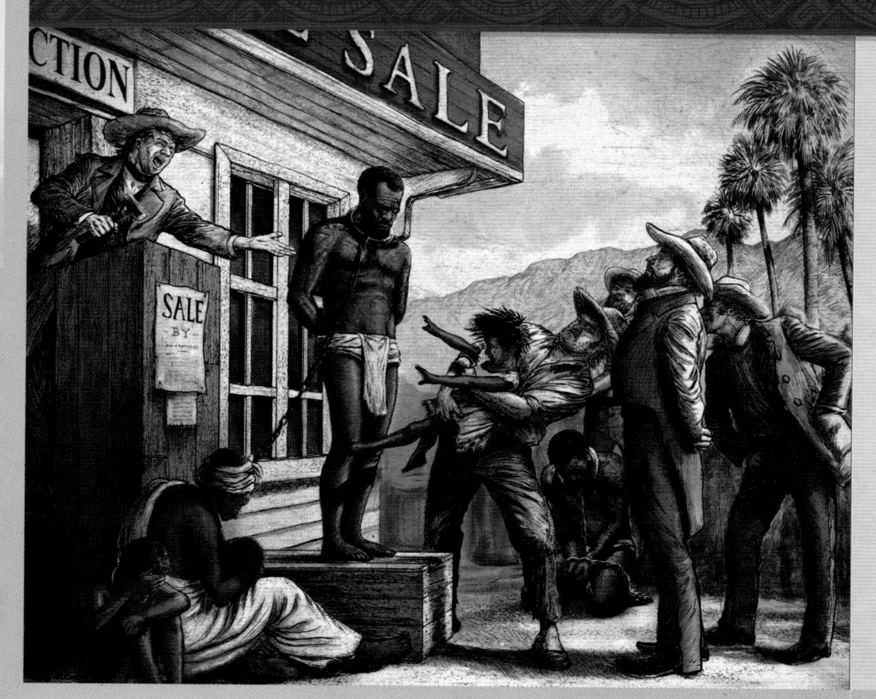

Ungodly PREJUDICE

Sadly, some professing Christians have misused passages of the Bible to spread racist ideas, such as slavery based on a person's skin tone or the notion that "interracial" marriage is sinful.

But what does the Bible really teach on these matters?

- **We are all created by God**— *Genesis 2:7*
- **We are all made in God's image**— *Genesis 1:26–27*
- **We are all one race**— *Acts 17:26*
- **We are all loved by God**— *John 3:16*

For God so loved the world, that He gave His only begotten Son, that whosoever believes in Him should not perish, but have everlasting life.

We are all descended from Adam, and later from Noah. As such, we are all members of the one human race.

SUPERFICIAL Biological DIFFERENCES

People GROUPS

Our superficial differences are merely the result of different combinations of features that humans have had since creation. The variety among different people groups could have occurred in a few generations in the small populations that split off from Babel.

If Noah and his wife had middle brown skin, their children could have exhibited the whole range of skin tones from light to dark.

Skin tone is governed by more than one gene. For simplicity, let's assume there are only two genes involved. Using a Punnett square, we can estimate the skin tones produced by a couple who both have middle brown skin and the genetic variability for light through dark skin.

\+ MELANIN −

MALE \ FEMALE	AB	Ab	aB	ab
AB	AABB	AABb	AaBB	AaBb
Ab	AABb	AAbb	AaBb	Aabb
aB	AaBB	AaBb	aaBB	aaBb
ab	AaBb	Aabb	aaBb	aabb

PEOPLE Groups AROUND the WORLD

One HUMAN RACE

From a biblical perspective, there is absolutely no basis for racism. God created mankind in His image. We are all descendants of Adam and Eve ***(Genesis 3:20)*** and are all part of the human race.

Then God said, "Let us make man in our image, in our likeness. And let them rule over the fish of the sea, over the birds of the sky, over the cattle, over all the earth, and over all the creatures that creep on the earth."

So God created man in His own image. In the image of God He created him; male and female He created them.

— Genesis 1:26–27 —

From one man He has made every nation of men to dwell on the face of the earth. He has determined their appointed times and the boundaries of their dwelling places.

— Acts 17:26 —

Different NATIONS

All the humans who settled the earth after the Flood descended from Noah's three sons. Yet the human gene pool split up after Babel. In just a few generations, varying combinations of previously existing genetic information resulted in distinct people groups, each with superficial differences, including different skin tones and eye shapes.

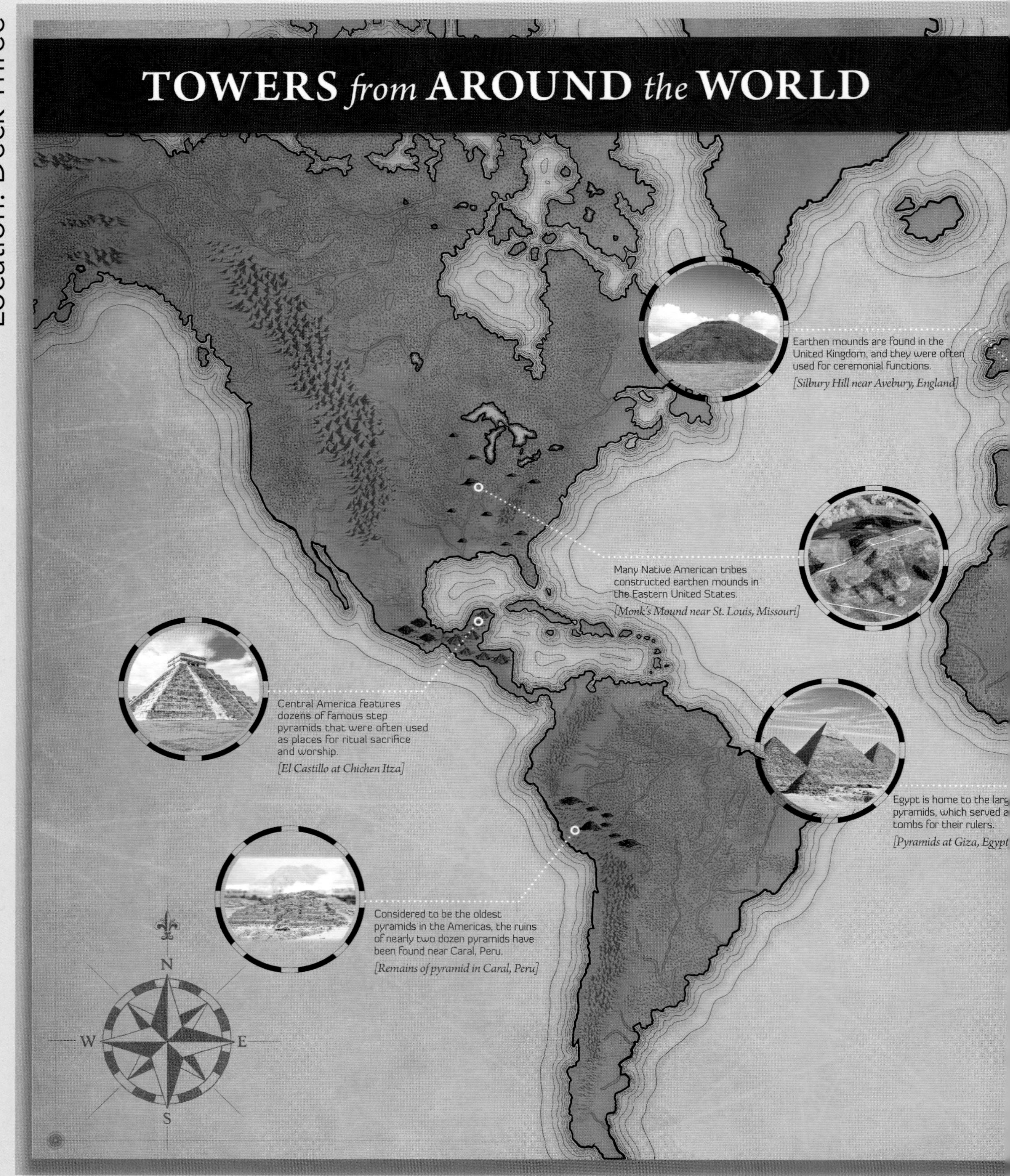
TOWERS from AROUND the WORLD
Earthen mounds are found in the United Kingdom, and they were often used for ceremonial functions.
[Silbury Hill near Avebury, England]
Many Native American tribes constructed earthen mounds in the Eastern United States.
[Monk's Mound near St. Louis, Missouri]
Central America features dozens of famous step pyramids that were often used as places for ritual sacrifice and worship.
[El Castillo at Chichen Itza]
Egypt is home to the larg
pyramids, which served a
tombs for their rulers.
[Pyramids at Giza, Egypt
Considered to be the oldest pyramids in the Americas, the ruins of nearly two dozen pyramids have been found near Caral, Peru.
[Remains of pyramid in Caral, Peru]
N
W
E
S

Roughly 100 earthen pyramids have been found in China. They were used as tombs for emperors and their relatives.
[The Anling Mausoleum in China]
Remains of Ziggurats are found throughout the area where Babel was located. Their names reveal that these structures were closely associated with the worship of the heavens.
[Great Ziggurat of Ur, Modern-day Iraq]
Smaller than their northern counterparts in Egypt, over 250 Nubian pyramids in Sudan were used as tombs.
[Nubian Pyramids near Meroe, Sudan]

The TOWERS

The Bible does not describe what the Tower of Babel looked like. Do the hundreds of ziggurats, pyramids, and earthen mounds from around the world provide clues about the tower's appearance and purpose?

Babel LEGENDS

Legends AROUND THE WORLD

The Bible accurately records the historical events at Babel. Some tribes have traditions that seem to describe the Babel event in their own way. These legends do not seem to be the result of missionary influence, as skeptics often allege. If they were truly handed down through the centuries, then we have some striking corroboration of the biblical account.

The Papago of Arizona—After a flood, the Great Spirit and Montezuma restocked the earth with men and animals. Montezuma became prideful and brought evil into the world when he rebelled against the Great Mystery by making the people build him a very tall house. The Great Mystery warned the people by raising the sun in the sky, which cooled the earth. He destroyed Montezuma's tower with an earthquake and changed the language of the people so that they could no longer understand the animals or other tribes.

The Mikir of Burma—In the old days, mighty giants ruled over the earth. They sought to conquer heaven so they built a tower to reach the skies. Fearing that the giants would take over, the gods confounded their speech and scattered them across the world.

The Choctaw of Southern United States—The first people wondered what the sky was like, so they decided to build a tower of rocks that would touch the heavens. After the wind destroyed their first two attempts, the people slept next to the tower on the third night. The tower was blown over again and the rocks landed on the people. When they pushed the rocks away, they were surprised to discover that they could no longer understand each other because they no longer spoke the same language.

ALIENS *and the* PYRAMIDS

Alien THINKING

Popular movies and television shows have suggested that these structures were either planned or built by aliens from outer space. But from a biblical perspective there is no basis for believing in extraterrestrials.

Even if we aren't fully sure how our predecessors accomplished these feats there is no need to appeal to alien involvement. Ancient man was highly intelligent and fully capable of constructing these engineering marvels. Our ancestors scattered from Babel, and the similarities in the design and purpose of these towers seem to reflect a common origin—***the Tower of Babel.***

TECHNOLOGY ·DOES NOT EQUAL· INTELLIGENCE

TECHNOLOGY IS THE PRACTICAL APPLICATION OF KNOWLEDGE.

Many people assume that since ancient cultures lacked our technological achievements, they must have been intellectually inferior. However, the ability to build a computer or smart phone does not make a person more intelligent than Albert Einstein (1879–1955) or Sir Isaac Newton (1643–1727).

"If I have seen further, it is by standing on the shoulders of giants."
—Sir Isaac Newton—

A culture's level of technology is not an accurate indicator of its intelligence. Technologies are often built upon the work of preceding generations. Early man did not possess our advanced technology, but we should not view our predecessors as less intelligent than we are. In fact, we can see evidence in the world around us that ancient people were highly intelligent.

PRE-FLOOD POTENTIAL

·MORE THAN CAPABLE·

HOW COULD NOAH BUILD SOMETHING SO LARGE AND SOPHISTICATED?

Many people believe that ancient man was not intelligent enough to design and build something as large and complex as the Ark, but they fail to consider some important details.

When Noah built the Ark, more than 1,600 years from Creation, his culture had made significant technological advances. The Bible does not tell us how advanced that civilization was, but we know they were fully capable of metalworking. There is no reason to think that they were not also highly proficient in using stone and wood for construction purposes.

WHICH VIEW IS CONFIRMED BY HISTORY AND ARCHAEOLOGY?

EVOLUTION

The popular view of our ancient ancestors has been strongly influenced by evolutionary teaching, which portrays early humans as unintelligent grunting brutes.

BIBLE

The Bible reveals that man was created in the image of God, and from the very beginning he was highly intelligent, capable of remarkable achievements.

DEVELOPING TECHNOLOGY

Genesis states that people in the pre-Flood world played musical instruments and worked with bronze and iron. We also know that Noah was capable of building the Ark. What other technologies might they have developed?

As people filled the earth certain innovations surely grew. Tools for farming and construction, along with roads and various means of transportation by land and water were surely invented. The longer lifespans could have enabled innovators and inventers to collaborate for decades, or even centuries, to produce sophisticated technologies.

1.1%*
GROWTH
PER YEAR
*CURRENT GROWTH RATE
1.2%
GROWTH
PER YEAR
1.3%
GROWTH
PER YEAR
1.4%
GROWTH
PER YEAR

HOW MANY PEOPLE LIVED ON EARTH PRIOR TO THE FLOOD?

POPULATION
147,551,508

Beginning with Adam and Eve and ending at the Flood, these calculations based on various growth rates estimate the number of people who lived before the Flood.

POPULATION: LOW OR HIGH?

The Bible does not reveal how many people existed before the Flood hit, so we can only make educated guesses.

POPULATION
758,505,443

Some people believe the population remained relatively low because the people were extremely corrupt and violent. The world may have been filled with wars, diseases, and other factors that kept the population in check.

POPULATION
3,892,884,443

Others believe that the population reached into the billions. With such long lifespans, families could have been very large, and the population growth rate may have been much higher than today.

Formula:

$$PF=PC\,(1+PGR)^n$$

POPULATION
19,947,270,231

(PF) Population before Flood= ?
(PC) Population at Creation= 2
(PGR) Population Growth Rate= 1.1%, 1.2%, 1.3%, 1.4%
(n) Years=1656 (approximate number of years before Flood)

TECHNOLOGICAL RESETS

From early history, men like Tubal-Cain worked with bronze and iron, but the Flood buried the sources of metal. As Noah's descendants populated the earth, metals needed to be rediscovered and technologies lost had to be reinvented.

Men began to rebuild, but they soon faced another technological setback—the judgment at Babel. As the various people groups scattered from that place, scientific achievements and technological advancements came slowly since most people spent their time struggling to meet their basic needs, such as food and shelter.

THE GREAT PYRAMID

•MONUMENTAL ACHIEVEMENT•

The only remaining building of the Seven Wonders of the Ancient World, the Great Pyramid of Giza is a massive engineering marvel. Built in the first few centuries after Babel, the precision in design as well as the sheer size of the pyramid have baffled researchers as they try to figure out how it was constructed.

- *Originally the pyramid stood over 480 feet tall (currently 455 feet)*
- *Base of the pyramid covers more than 13 acres and is within 15mm of being perfectly flat*
- *All four base sides are approximately 755.9 feet long, varying by an average of just two inches*
- *An estimated 2,400,000 stones weighing an average of 2.5 tons make up the pyramid*
- *Stood as the tallest building in the world for over 3,000 years*

THE ENIGMATIC STONEHENGE

·MOVING MEGALITHS·

One of the most recognizable landmarks in the world, Stonehenge is another engineering marvel constructed without the use of modern technology. Early settlers of England moved these huge rocks, called megaliths, into place and arranged the stones to align with the sunrise of the summer solstice and sunset of the winter solstice.

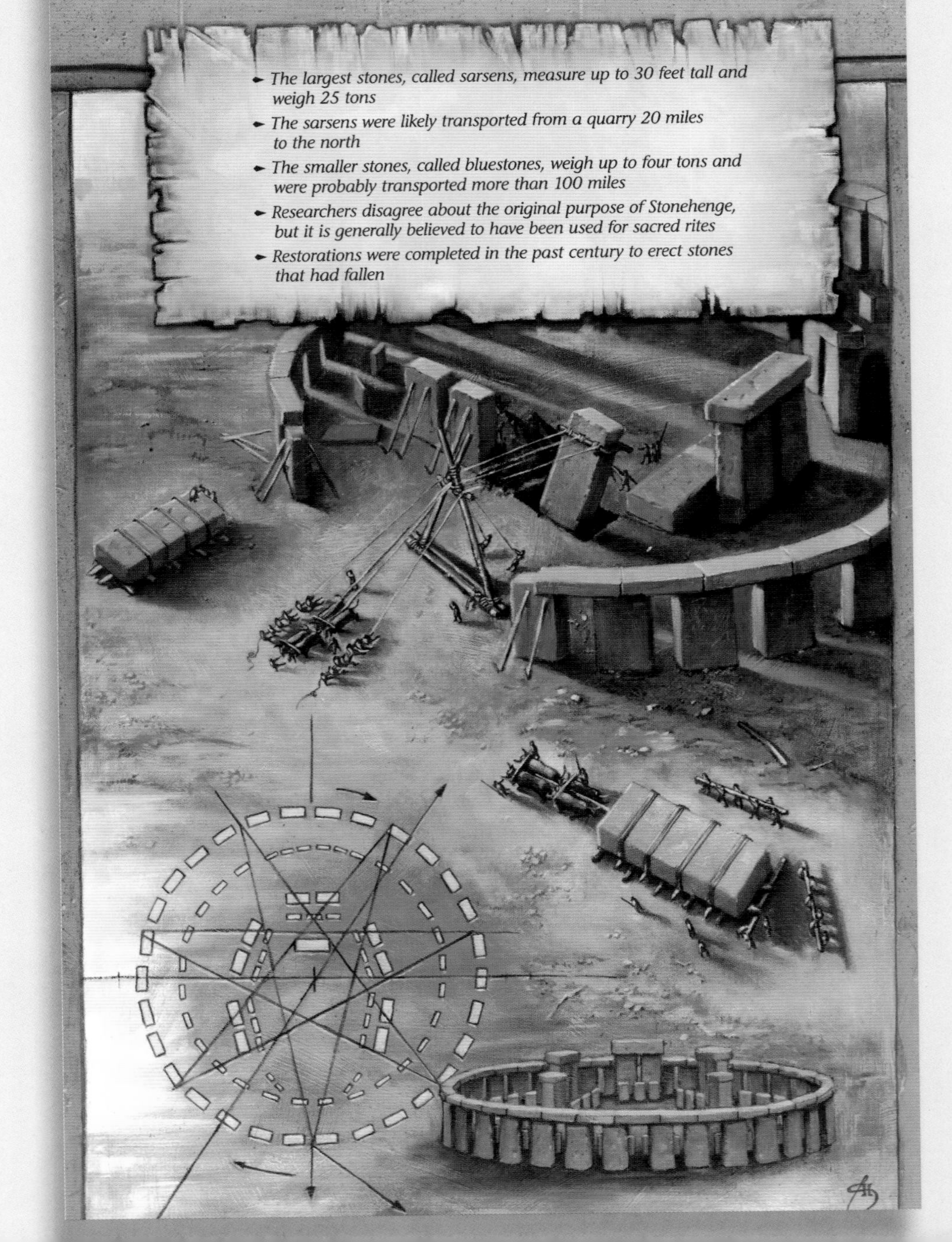

The largest stones, called sarsens, measure up to 30 feet tall and weigh 25 tons
The sarsens were likely transported from a quarry 20 miles to the north
The smaller stones, called bluestones, weigh up to four tons and were probably transported more than 100 miles
Researchers disagree about the original purpose of Stonehenge, but it is generally believed to have been used for sacred rites
Restorations were completed in the past century to erect stones that had fallen

TIME AND NAVIGATION

· ASTRONOMICAL INTELLIGENCE ·

The intelligence of early humans is demonstrated through their understanding and use of astronomical observations for timekeeping and navigation. The incredibly precise Mayan calendar is probably the best known of these ancient devices, but many sites and artifacts dating back to the second millennium BC have been discovered around the world that display our ancestors' ingenuity.

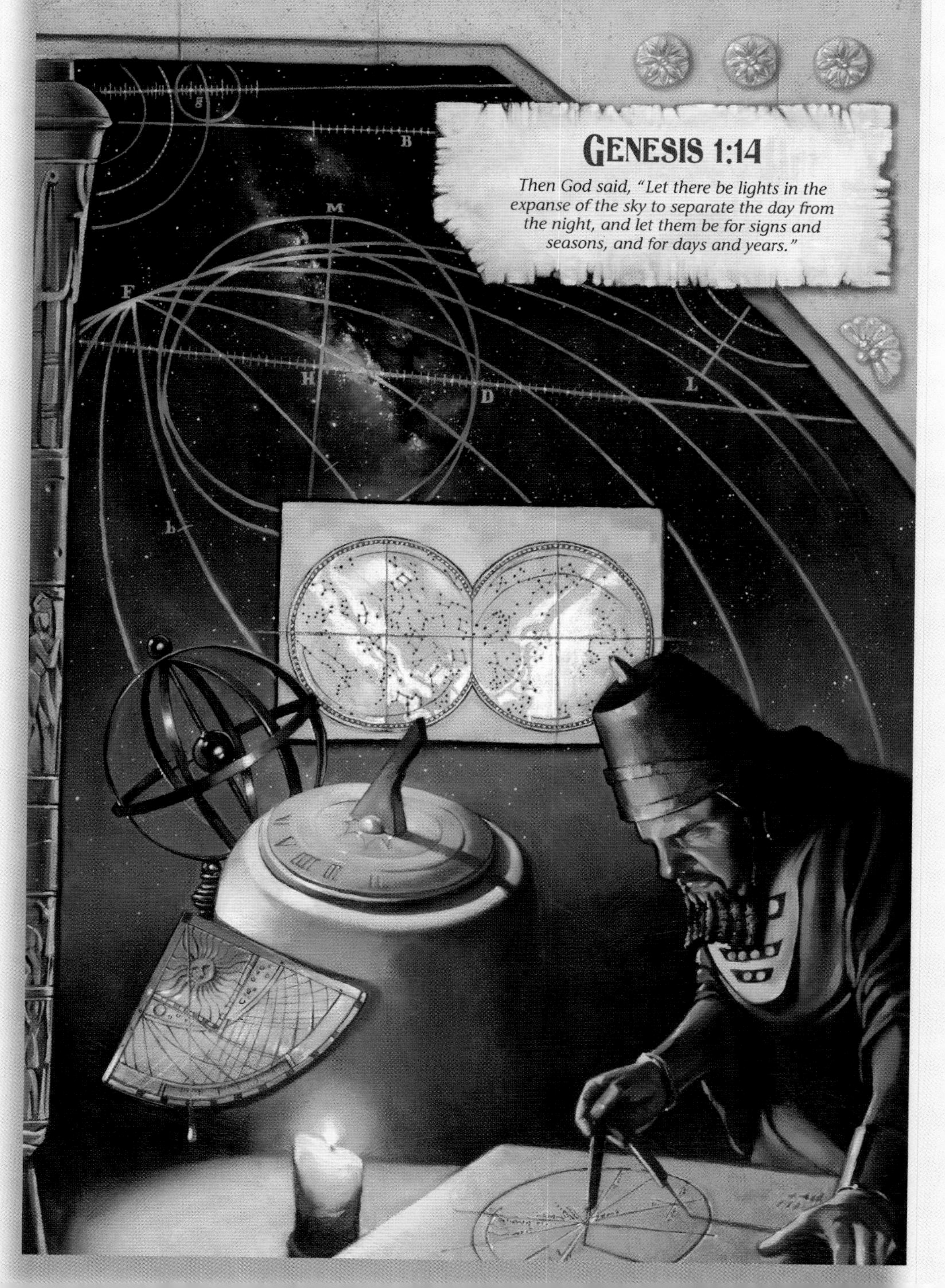

GENESIS 1:14
Then God said, "Let there be lights in the expanse of the sky to separate the day from the night, and let them be for signs and seasons, and for days and years."

AN INTELLIGENT LOOK AT ANCIENT MAN

The evolutionary story often portrays ancient man as a brutish caveman. Over the years, he evolved to become a hunter-gatherer. During the "Agricultural Revolution" these hunter-gatherers became farmers and raised flocks. Eventually, men advanced to the point that they began to build cities.

Once again, the biblical account of man makes better sense of what we have observed. The caveman, hunter-gatherer, farmer, and city-builder definitely existed, but they all existed at the same time. In fact, each of these types of people can be found in the world today.

Rather than reflecting an evolutionary progression of early man, these different societies are consistent with what we would expect to find following the Babel incident. People scattered from Babel, bringing their own set of skills to the areas they settled. Some areas were more favorable for hunting while others were better for farming. Certain groups spent much of their time scraping out a living trying to find enough food for the day, while societies that produced an abundance of food could devote time to developing their technology.

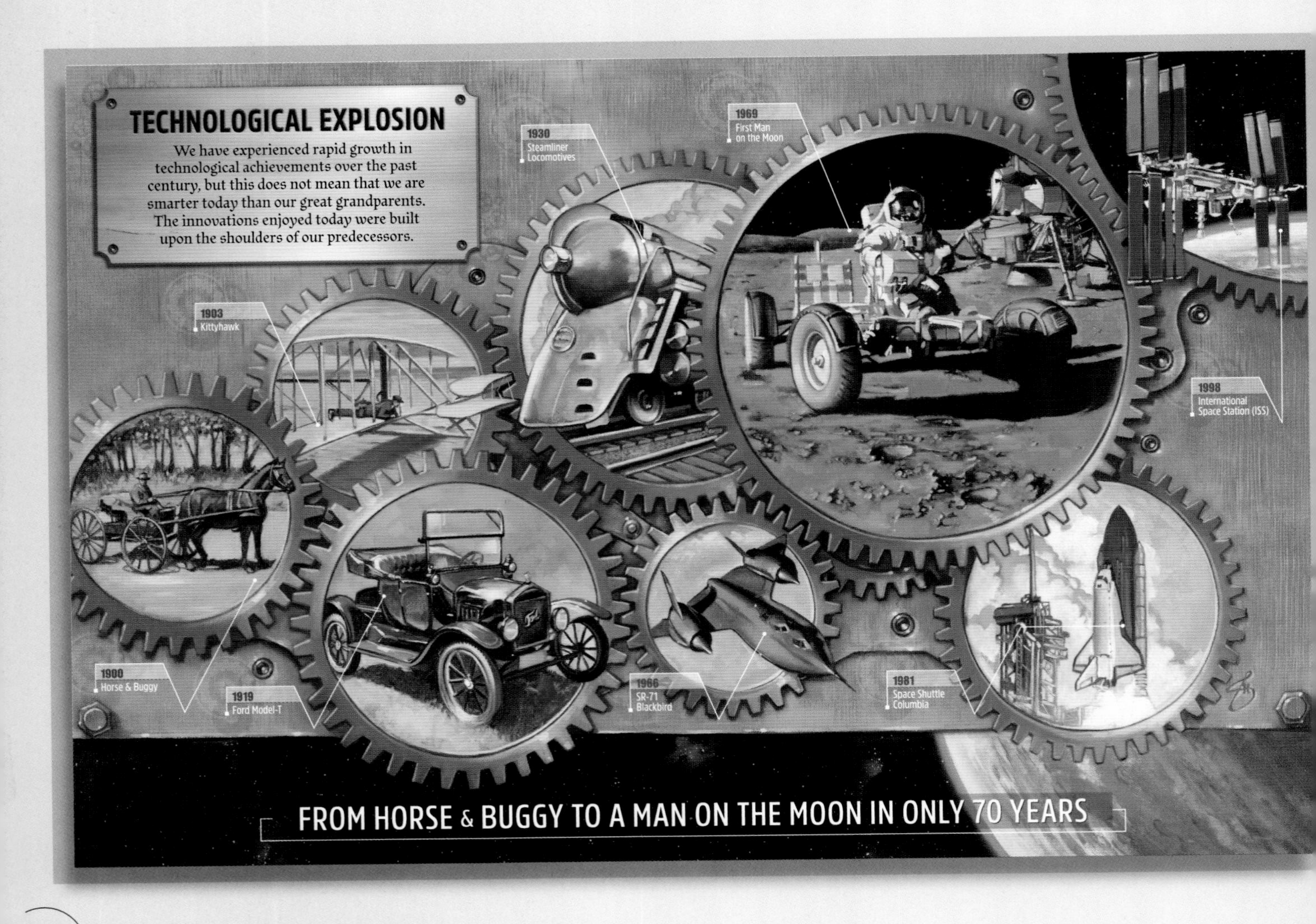
TECHNOLOGICAL EXPLOSION
We have experienced rapid growth in technological achievements over the past century, but this does not mean that we are smarter today than our great grandparents. The innovations enjoyed today were built upon the shoulders of our predecessors.
1930 Steamliner Locomotives
1969 First Man on the Moon
1903 Kittyhawk
1998 International Space Station (ISS)
1900 Horse & Buggy
1919 Ford Model-T
1966 SR-71 Blackbird
1981 Space Shuttle Columbia
FROM HORSE & BUGGY TO A MAN ON THE MOON IN ONLY 70 YEARS

·FALSE VIEWS ABOUT ANCIENT MAN·

APE ANCESTRY

Evolutionists claim that man descended from ape-like ancestors, but no intermediate fossils have ever been found to verify this idea. The so-called "missing links" between ape-like creatures and humans were either fully ape (e.g., Lucy and Ardipithecus), fully man (e.g., Neanderthals and Cro-Magnon), or complete frauds (e.g., Nebraska Man and Piltdown Man).

The Bible is clear that God made man from the dust of the ground, and woman was made from his rib. There are no ape-like creatures in our ancestry.

PREHISTORIC

The concept of "prehistoric" events, animals, and people contradicts the biblical worldview. *Prehistoric* means "before history," and refers to a time when man was either not around or was incapable of keeping records of his world. But man was made on Day Six. He was fully capable of keeping a record of events through oral or written testimonies and passing on those details to the following generations. The first five days could not really be considered prehistoric since God revealed the history of what He did on those days. So the concept of prehistoric does not make sense from a biblical perspective.

A FLAT EARTH

The popular myth that ancient peoples believed the earth is flat was popularized in the late 19th century by John Draper and Andrew Dickson White. These men sought to belittle Christians by making the Medieval church look ignorant and anti-science. In reality, people have long known the earth was round. In the third century BC, Eratosthenes calculated the circumference of the earth to within one percent. The Bible also includes passages that imply a round earth.

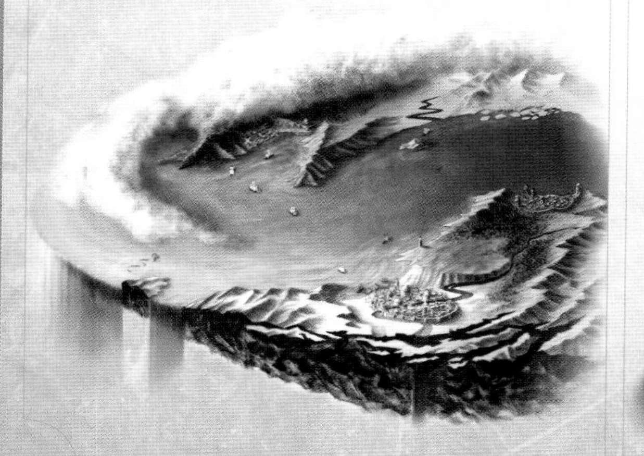

EVOLUTION OF RELIGION

Many people assume that humanity's religious beliefs began with a form of animism or spiritism. Eventually, these beliefs gave way to polytheism (belief in many gods) and then to monotheism (belief in one all-powerful God). However, the Bible explains, and historical studies have confirmed, that the opposite is true. Man began with a belief in the one true God, but knowledge of the Creator diminished in many cultures, giving rise to the false views of polytheism, animism, and spiritism.

FLOODED WITH LEGENDS

OVER 200 LEGENDS OF an ancient global flood have been discovered around the world. These legends vary in their level of consistency with the biblical account, yet certain details are widely distributed. For example, many of these tales speak of a favored family who built a huge boat and, along with some animals, survived a worldwide catastrophe sent by an angry deity.

WHAT IS THE BEST explanation for the existence of these Flood legends? Are they merely unrelated tales of local catastrophes endured by each culture's ancestors? Are they simply recountings of a myth spread in ancient history? The best explanation fits the Bible perfectly: the people who split from Babel passed on their knowledge of the biblical Flood, but their stories became distorted during many centuries of retellings.

Critics of the Bible often claim that the biblical Flood account was copied from ancient Babylonian or Sumerian flood legends since these writings predate the time of Moses. However, it makes much more sense to believe the biblical account reveals the true history of the Flood while the legends tell a distorted version of the same event.

1.

Since the Bible is God's Word, it is accurate in all that it records. This accuracy is not limited to matters of faith, but includes every subject the Bible addresses, including history.

2.

Only the dimensions of the biblical Ark provide the ideal size, strength, stability, and comfort for a ship built to protect the people and animals during the Flood.

3.

Many flood legends highlight a mountain, animals, and boat structure common to the people of the region. However, the Bible does not localize the event.

Did MISSIONARIES GIVE RISE to the various Flood legends?

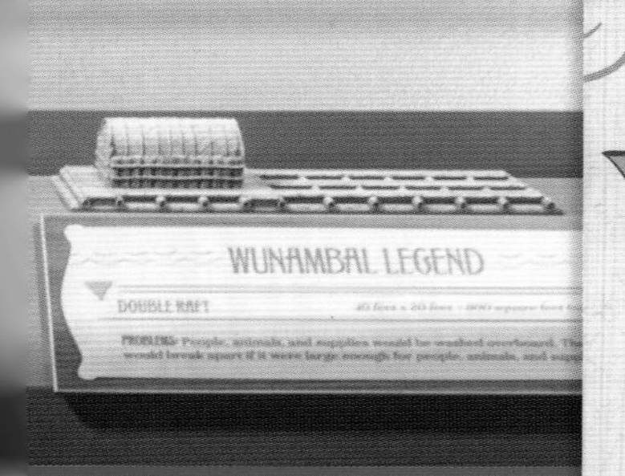

WUNAMBAL LEGEND

DOUBLE RAFT *40 feet x 20 feet = 800 square feet (one level)*

PROBLEMS: People, animals, and supplies would be washed overboard. The raft would break apart if it were large enough for people, animals, and supplies.

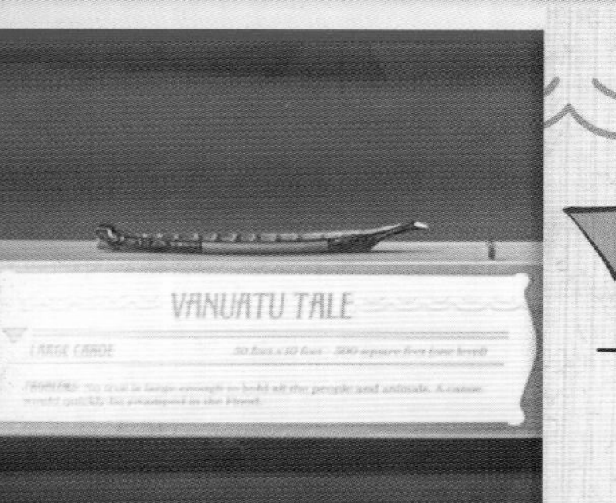

VANUATU TALE

LARGE CANOE *50 feet x 10 feet = 500 square feet (one level)*

PROBLEMS: No tree is large enough to hold all the people and animals. A canoe would quickly be swamped in the Flood.

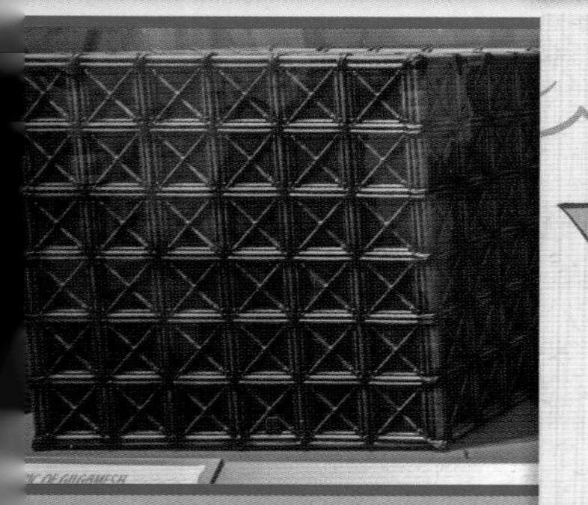

EPIC OF GILGAMESH

CUBE-SHAPED ARK *204 feet x 204 feet = 291,312 square feet (seven levels)*

PROBLEMS: Lighting and ventilation for lower decks. Tilting and rocking in waves would make voyage virtually unbearable.

SOME CRITICS WHO ARE SKEPTICAL about the Flood being a global event will state that the reason so many flood legends exist is due to the influence of Christian missionaries over the centuries. While this rationale may explain a handful of the accounts, it fails in the vast majority of cases.

1.

MANY FLOOD LEGENDS were written long before any interaction with Christian missionaries.

2.

THE MANY DIFFERENCES between the legends and Genesis show that these cultures were not simply repeating what Christian missionaries had taught. Instead, they were embellishing history.

3.

OTHER BIBLICAL EVENTS that occurred prior to the dispersion at Babel are often found among these legends, but they make no mention of later biblical events. Principally, there is no mention of Jesus Christ.

WHY WOULD MISSIONARIES spend their lives with unreached people groups to share distorted versions of the Flood without ever teaching people about the forgiveness of sins available in Jesus?

AKKADIAN TABLET

LARGE CORACLE

220 feet diameter = 38,013 square feet (one level)

PROBLEMS: Sides are too short to prevent waves from washing over and sinking the boat. Reeds and rope would not be strong enough to support the massive structure and pressure from the waves.

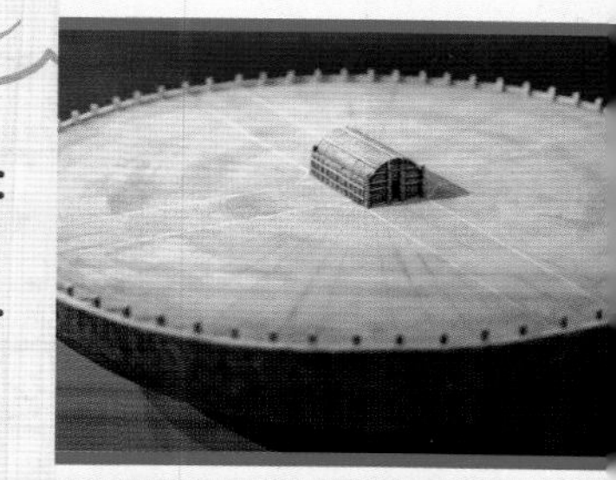

THE BIBLE

NOAH'S ARK

510 feet x 85 feet = 110,540 square feet (three levels)

PROBLEMS: None, it was perfectly designed to survive the Flood.
STRENGTHS: Large enough for all of the animals, people, and supplies. Dimensions are an ideal blend for strength, stability, and comfort.

Exhibit: **Rainbow Covenant**

Location: Deck Three

And God Blessed Them

Genesis 9:1

Image Bearers

Although man was corrupt, the Lord reiterated that man is still made in God's image, and thus all human life is of immeasurable value.

Dominion

God said that all of the animals were placed under man's authority, reflecting His directive to man in the Garden of Eden.

Marriage

Similar to the Lord's blessing on man in Genesis 1, He instructed Noah and his family to be fruitful and multiply, and fill the earth.

Capital Punishment

God said to Noah, "I will demand an account for your life…Whoever spills man's blood by man shall his blood be spilled, because in the image of God He made man." (Genesis 9:5–6)

God stressed the value of human life by sanctioning the death penalty for acts of murder. If a person murders another human being, he has destroyed someone made in the image of God, which is a grave offense against the Lord Himself. Other serious crimes were also deemed worthy of capital punishment under the Law of Moses, and the New Testament states that governing authorities have the right to execute judgment for such crimes (Romans 13:4).

Permission to Eat Meat

"Every beast of the earth and every bird of the sky will be afraid of you. Every creeping thing on the ground and all the fish of the sea are given into your hands. Just as I previously gave you all the green plants for food, I now give you all things: every moving and living thing shall be food for you. But you shall not eat flesh with its life, that is, its blood." (Genesis 9:3–4)

Dietary Changes

In the beginning, God gave man authority over the beasts of the earth, birds of the air, and fish of the sea. After the Flood, He gave Noah and his sons a similar blessing along with a significant difference.

Originally man was only allowed to eat vegetation (Genesis 1:29). However, when the Flood ended, God gave man permission to eat meat with the qualification that it did not have its lifeblood in it. God would later restrict certain meats under His covenant with the Israelites at Mt. Sinai, but the New Testament shows that these restrictions were intended for a certain people at a certain time.

Noahic Covenant

And Noah built an altar to the Lord, and he took from all the clean animals and clean birds and sacrificed them as burnt offerings on the altar. God smelled the pleasing aroma and said, "I will never again…destroy all of the life which I have made. As long as the earth remains, seedtime and harvest, cold and heat, summer and winter, and day and night will not cease." (Genesis 8:20–22)

The Covenant

God spoke to Noah and his sons saying, "I am about to confirm My covenant with you and with all of your descendants, and with all the living things that are with you." (Genesis 9:8–10)

Following the sacrifice Noah made, God established a covenant with both man and animals. He promised to **never again** bring a global flood to wipe out all life from the earth.

Rainbow Sign

And God said, "This is the sign of the covenant…I will place My rainbow in the clouds and it shall be a sign of the covenant between Me and the earth." (Genesis 9:12–13)

The Lord used the rainbow as a sign of His promise that He would **never again** flood the entire earth. Each rainbow is a reminder of God's promise to all living things.

God's Character

"And whenever I bring clouds above the earth and My rainbow appears, I will remember My covenant between Me and you and every living thing." (Genesis 9:14–15)

God has established His reputation on His ability to fulfill His promises. If the Flood in the days of Noah were merely a regional event, rather than global, then with every local flood the Lord has broken His promise to **never again** flood the earth.

Here one can see the progress being made as the Amish team puts together more bents. The first one took two weeks to assemble and raise into place. They were eventually able to do two in a week's time.

The Ark construction with six bents fully in place.

Now with 15 bents in place, and starting on the outer skin as well.

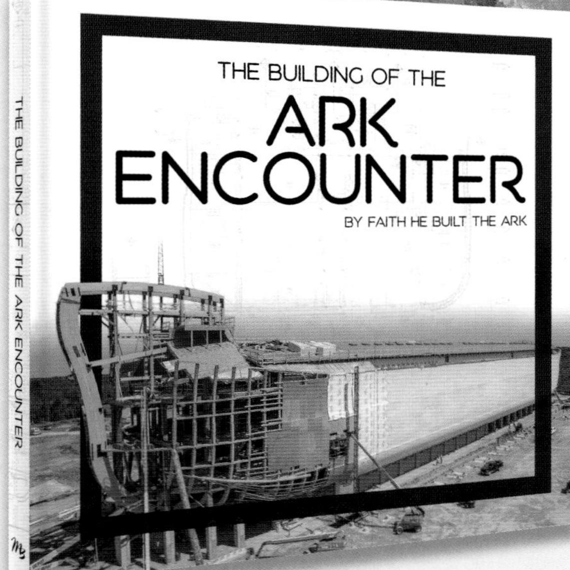

Discover details of this engineering masterpiece as the largest timberframed building in the world. At 510 feet long, 85 feet wide, and 51 feet high based on the Bible's dimensions, it presents the world with an awe-inspiring reminder of the scriptural account of the Ark.

$17.99 U.S.
C 978-0-89051-931-8

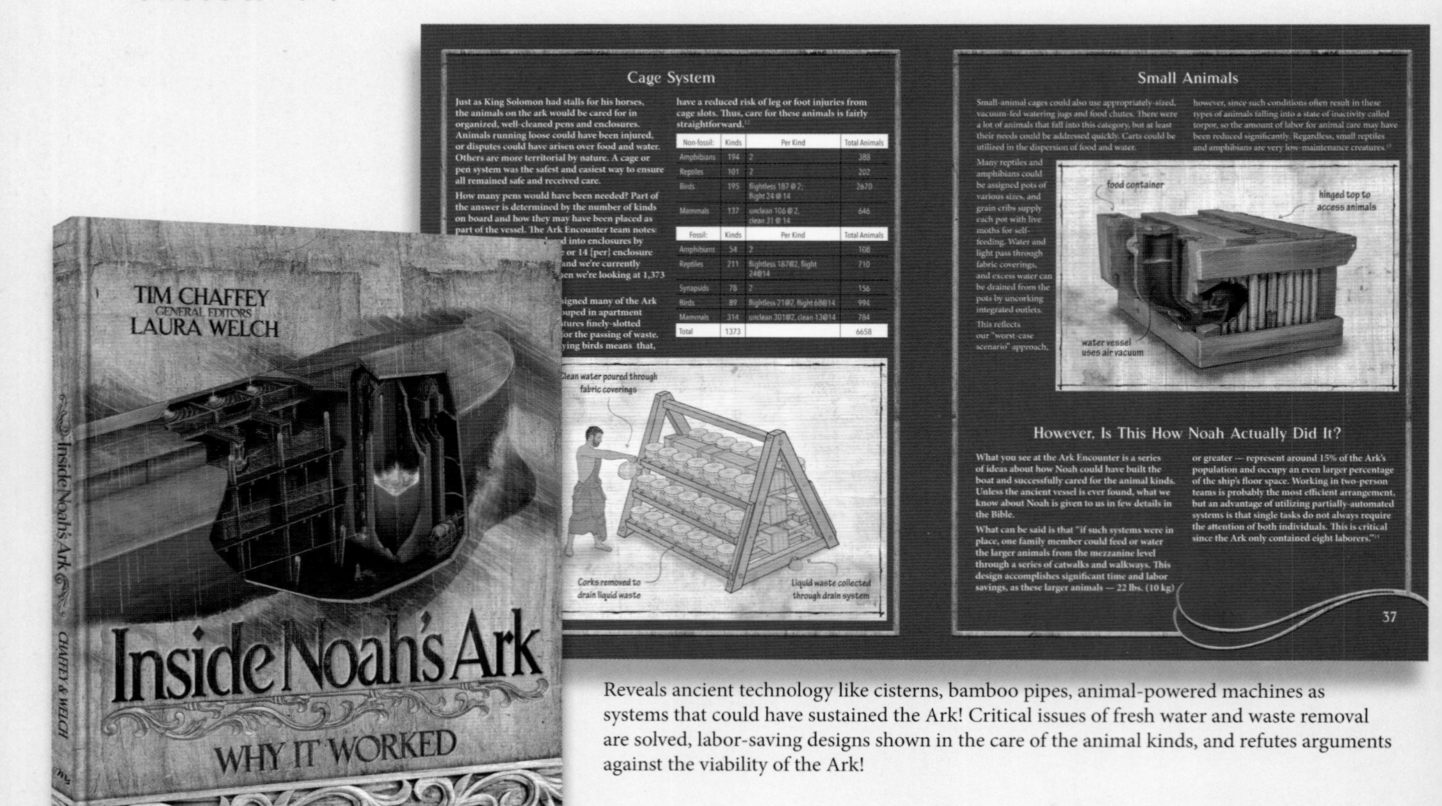

Cage System

Just as King Solomon had stalls for his horses, the animals on the ark would be cared for in organized, well-cleaned pens and enclosures. Animals running loose could have been injured, or disputes could have arisen over food and water. Others are more territorial by nature. A cage or pen system was the safest and easiest way to ensure all remained safe and received care.

How many pens would have been needed? Part of the answer is determined by the number of kinds on board and how they may have been placed as part of the vessel. The Ark Encounter team notes: ... d into enclosures by ... or 14 [per] enclosure ... and we're currently ... en we're looking at 1,373 ...

... signed many of the Ark ... ouped in apartment ... tures finely-slotted ... for the passing of waste. ... ying birds means that, have a reduced risk of leg or foot injuries from cage slots. Thus, care for these animals is fairly straightforward.[12]

Non-fossil:	Kinds	Per Kind	Total Animals
Amphibians	194	2	388
Reptiles	101	2	202
Birds	195	flightless 187 @ 2; flight 24 @ 14	2670
Mammals	137	unclean 106 @ 2, clean 31 @ 14	646
Fossil:	**Kinds**	**Per Kind**	**Total Animals**
Amphibians	54	2	108
Reptiles	211	flightless 187@2, flight 24@14	710
Synapsids	78	2	156
Birds	89	flightless 21@2, flight 68@14	994
Mammals	314	unclean 301@2, clean 13@14	784
Total	1373		6658

Small Animals

Small-animal cages could also use appropriately-sized, vacuum-fed watering jugs and food chutes. There were a lot of animals that fall into this category, but at least their needs could be addressed quickly. Carts could be utilized in the dispersion of food and water.

Many reptiles and amphibians could be assigned pots of various sizes, and grain cribs supply each pot with live moths for self-feeding. Water and light pass through fabric coverings, and excess water can be drained from the pots by uncorking integrated outlets.

This reflects our "worst-case scenario" approach, however, since such conditions often result in these types of animals falling into a state of inactivity called torpor, so the amount of labor for animal care may have been reduced significantly. Regardless, small reptiles and amphibians are very low-maintenance creatures.[13]

However, Is This How Noah Actually Did It?

What you see at the Ark Encounter is a series of ideas about how Noah could have built the boat and successfully cared for the animal kinds. Unless the ancient vessel is ever found, what we know about Noah is given to us in few details in the Bible.

What can be said is that "if such systems were in place, one family member could feed or water the larger animals from the mezzanine level through a series of catwalks and walkways. This design accomplishes significant time and labor savings, as these larger animals — 22 lbs. (10 kg) or greater — represent around 15% of the Ark's population and occupy an even larger percentage of the ship's floor space. Working in two-person teams is probably the most efficient arrangement, but an advantage of utilizing partially-automated systems is that single tasks do not always require the attention of both individuals. This is critical since the Ark only contained eight laborers."[14]

37

Reveals ancient technology like cisterns, bamboo pipes, animal-powered machines as systems that could have sustained the Ark! Critical issues of fresh water and waste removal are solved, labor-saving designs shown in the care of the animal kinds, and refutes arguments against the viability of the Ark!

$16.99 U.S.
C 978-0-89051-932-5

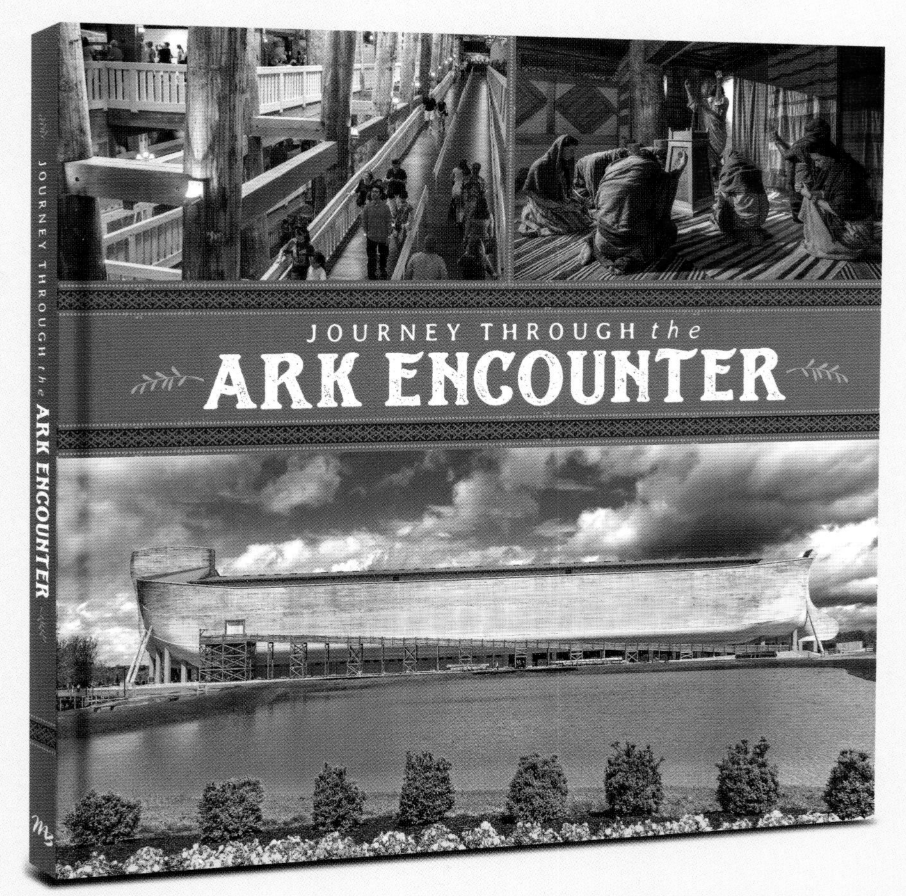

$24.99 U.S.
C 978-1-68344-012-3

Step back in time and explore one of the best-known biblical events at the Ark Encounter! Take an amazing tour of this remarkable, life size replica of Noah's Ark through the pages of this book and learn about the world's true history that is shared through unique, world-class exhibits.

JOURNEY THROUGH the ARK ENCOUNTER

DECK TWO

Animal Care

This extremely popular exhibit explores questions that most people have never considered. How could the small cages be designed to minimize precious time for feeding and cleaning up after the animals? How were small reptiles and amphibians housed and fed? How did Noah's family provide for animals with picky diets, such as koalas and anteaters?

The second bay of this exhibit focuses on some large-scale issues concerning the Ark. How could Noah's family collect enough water for drinking and cleaning? How was the Ark ventilated and lit? How could they efficiently remove waste?

Dioramas and interactive videos demonstrate possible techniques used on the Ark to automate some of the daily chores involved in caring for a large number of animals.

42

43